Outreach Promises

GOD'S ENCOURAGEMENT FOR SHARING YOUR FAITH

PHILIP M. BICKEL

Roller Coaster Press
St. Paul, Minnesota

Published by Roller Coaster Press
1167 Ryan Avenue W., Roseville, Minnesota 55113-5929

Patterson Printing, 1550 Territorial Road, Benton Harbor, MI 49022

Cover design and illustrations by Susan B. Crawford.

Library of Congress Catalog Card Number: 98-91364
ISBN 0-9663765-0-1
Subjects: 1. Evangelistic work. 2. Missions. 3. Biblical theology.

Acknowledgements

I thank God for:
- The audiences who permitted me to speak and teach about outreach promises.
- Those who previewed the manuscript and offered expert advice: Peter and Betty Cook, Ralph Geisler, Keith and Miriam Haney, Roger Greenway, Joel Heck, David Hesselgrave, Herb Hoefer, Phil Johnson, Jerry Kosberg, Karen Merkel, Carl Selle, Timothy Warner, Joan Webb, and Scott Zimmerman.
- World Mission Prayer League and Raquel Lundberg for typesetting assistance.
- My wife, Julie, who has helped me process this topic for years.

Dedication

To Christian witnesses and missionaries around the world
who long for words of encouragement.

CONTENTS

INTRODUCTION

DESIGN AND USE OF THIS BOOK

Purpose and goal. If you like sharing your faith in Christ, you will like this book. If you find witnessing and mission work difficult, you might love this book.

The concept of outreach promises is both ancient and brand new. Outreach promises have been in the Bible all along, and yet to many Christians they will seem new, because we tend to overlook them.

The purpose of *Outreach Promises* is to introduce you to this new/ancient category of Bible promises. The goal is that you will learn to lean on these promises and trust in the Lord whenever you have opportunity to serve and speak in the name of Christ.

Dialogue and discovery. A book ought to be a dialogue between the author and the reader. Please don't merely read this book. Interact with it. To enable dialogue, the text is peppered with reflective questions. These questions are your opportunity to interact with me. Your half of the discussion is every bit as important as mine.

Some questions are multiple choice. Others require more thought. When you see the pencil symbol, ✏️▷, that means you are invited to jot down a response. Whether you write anything and how much you write is your choice.

Even though questions appear in the text, *Outreach Promises* is not a workbook. It is a discoverybook. What's the difference?

Many workbooks are busy work, designed for readers to parrot back what has been taught. A discoverybook helps you process and appraise new ideas. Workbooks which expect pat, predictable answers often bore people. Questions in a discoverybook make you think—and pray. Some workbooks have an answer key in the back of the book. The answers for this book are found within you, as the Holy Spirit guides you. The art of teaching is the art of assisting discovery. That is why *Outreach Promises* is designed as a discoverybook.

Structure and reading styles. Seven chapters develop the concept of outreach promises. Each chapter consists of five sections which average about two pages in length.

Appendix 1 contains a group discussion guide. Appendix 2 will help you find outreach promises in your Bible.

Because everyone has their own preferred way to read a book, *Outreach Promises* permits a variety of reading styles.

Option 1. You can read it as a devotional book with enough material for thirty-five quiet times with the Lord. Each two-page section concludes with a brief prayer and a suggested action to take in response to the message.

Option 2. You can read straight through with few pauses or distractions. Take a moment to look at the questions, but don't worry about writing responses. Later, you may review those sections and questions that seem most interesting to you.

Option 3. You can read at a moderate, thoughtful pace, pausing wherever you like, giving yourself time to ponder the new ideas and questions.

Option 4. With the help of Appendix 1, you can study the book with a Bible study group. Read a chapter before each small group session, reflect on the questions, and then discuss the contents with others.

Near and far. Sharing our joy in the Lord with unbelievers is the privilege of Christians in all lands. Wherever we live, we face similar challenges and fears. For this reason, the text includes true stories and fictional vignettes from around the world. These examples reveal how much we have in common. *Outreach Promises* is easily readable for English-speaking audiences in any nation, because only widely familiar metaphors and illustrations appear in the text. As a result, the book is readily translatable into other languages.

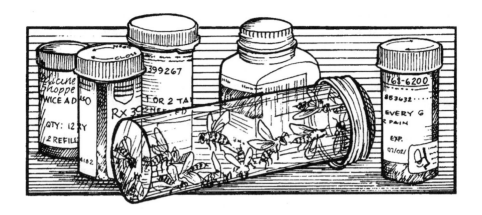

1   GOOD STINGS FOR CHRISTIAN OUTREACH

This chapter explains why you and all Christians need the assurance and encouragement of God's outreach promises.

A. Could You Use a Good Sting?

A bizarre remedy. Seated in her motorized wheel chair, Bette gazes through her living room window. Over the years multiple sclerosis has progressively attacked her nervous system, restricting her mobility and almost paralyzing her limbs. Two years ago she had to give up walking with a cane and accept the assistance of her mobile chair.

With difficulty Bette lifts her arm. She senses her strength waning. If she doesn't act soon, she won't be able to manipulate the controls of the wheel chair. From her pocket she lifts a vial. It seems to be buzzing. Carefully, she removes from the vial a honey bee pinched between her thumb and forefinger. Then she intentionally allows the bee to sting her on the forearm.

"Ahh, that's better," Bette says. "All I needed was a good sting."

This bizarre remedy actually works. Bee venom counteracts the debilitating symptoms of diseases like multiple sclerosis and arthritis. When sufferers feel their mobility diminishing, they grab a bee and give themselves a good sting.

If you fear bee stings, this remedy might make you cringe. However, if you were barely able to move, you probably would appreciate the benefits of a good sting.

A divine remedy. God has a vision to reach a lost world with the gospel of Christ. However, most Christians have difficulty witnessing even to their own family, good friends, and neighbors. Evangelizing a spiritist, a Muslim, or a Buddhist can seem nearly impossible. Such challenges often leave us paralyzed by outreach doubts, fears, and discouragement. We need a good sting.

Wouldn't it be great, if God—knowing our reluctance and discouragement—had assured us repeatedly he would bless our efforts to proclaim the gospel to our neighbors and all the world? He did! In the Bible He gave us hundreds of outreach promises. These often-overlooked promises are "good stings."

For many believers, their attitude and motivation regarding evangelism is command-oriented. "Christians should witness and do mission work," they say, "because God told us to. So let's get moving!" But what would happen if our attitude and motivation were more promise-oriented? To inform us what to do, God gave us outreach *commands*. To encourage and empower us to obey the commands, He gave us outreach *promises*.

Would you like to use them as God intended?

Paul the Missionary understood outreach promises. As he strove to shine the gospel light in dark places, he clung to this promise: "Those who were not told about him will see, and those who have not heard will understand" (Rom. 15:21). This is a quote from Isaiah 52:15. Isaiah also understood outreach promises. In fact, by the Holy Spirit's inspiration, Isaiah authored more outreach promises than any other Old Testament writer.

Jesus also knew the power of God's promises to encourage our compassionate service and witness. That's why He assured us with statements like, "You are the light of the world. A city on a hill cannot be hidden" (Mt. 5:14).

The theme of this book is: In the same way that gospel promises contain the power to produce faith in Christ and convert us, so God's outreach promises create within us faith in God's ability to carry out His mission through us.

The goal of this book is to teach you how to recognize outreach promises and put them to use as you share your faith.

Discovery. What is your reaction so far to this new idea?

___ a. What is this guy talking about? I don't get it.

___ b. It sounds good, but to be convinced I need to hear more.

___ c. It speaks to a hunger I've felt, but never could satisfy.

Prayer: Lord, help me grasp hold of Your outreach promises.

Action: Tell others about the healing power of bee venom. Ask if they could use a good sting to help share their faith.

B. Clarify and Personalize

Clear definitions. Allow me to define five basic terms. Some Christians have a negative attitude toward them. I hope by the end of this book your attitude will be positive.

1. Evangelism. "Evangel" means good news. The Christmas angel announced to the shepherds, "Do not be afraid. I bring you good news of great joy that will be for all people" (Lk. 2:10). The good news of the Bible is that Jesus Christ has won salvation for us by offering Himself for our sins on the cross of Calvary and rising from the dead. What news could be better than this?

Many people have a narrow view of evangelism. Some think it refers solely to gospel crusades or church calling programs or approaching total strangers with questions about their eternal destiny. Evangelism is wider than all these. It includes any and all methods Christians use to invite people to repent of their sins and believe the good news of what Christ has done to redeem them.

2. Personal witnessing. Peter describes personal witnessing in 1 Pt. 3:15. "Always be prepared to give an answer to everyone who asks you to give the reason for the hope that you have. But do this with gentleness and respect...." Witnessing occurs in everyday conversations whenever we tell what Christ has done for us. We need to avoid the trap of making witnessing more complicated than it is. Place a ✔ by any of the expectations below which you have held. Are they realistic or unrealistic?

___ a. I should have the answer to every question I am asked.

___ b. I must accurately quote Bible verses from memory.

___ c. I ought to teach people every key doctrine in one sitting.

___ d. I dare not make a single mistake.

___ e. If I don't lead the person to Christ today, I have failed.

Feel free to drop all these unnecessary burdens from your weary back. Your duty as a witness is only this: To tell how God has had mercy on you and to leave the results to Him.

3. Mission. Ultimately, the good news is for every man, woman, and child on earth. To reach all those different and dis-

tant people is the mission Christ gave us. Those who proclaim Christ in a culture other than their own are called missionaries.

4. World evangelization. This is the ultimate goal of God's global mission. We are called to announce the good news to every tribe, language, people, and nation. Please note, world evangelization does not mean that everyone will *believe* the message of salvation, but that the message will *be proclaimed* to everyone. When this is accomplished, then the Great Commission, "to make disciples of all nations" (Mt. 28:19), will be fulfilled.

5. Christian outreach. This broad term includes all the items defined above: evangelism, witnessing, mission, and world evangelization. In those definitions I stressed communicating the good news of Christ verbally, but is Christian outreach only verbal? Not at all. Many activities enhance our verbal witness. These include: friendship, love, caring for people in need, and acts of compassion, mercy, and justice. Such activities are linked with speaking the good news, in order that people may come to know and trust the one, true God who calls them into a saving relationship with Himself.

Clear objectives. Okay, I have clarified some things. Now it is time for you to do the same. Reflect on the questions below. They will help you personalize this book and discover ways to apply the hope of outreach promises to your life. You may elect to pass over these questions and keep on reading. If so, please remember the questions still are calling your name. The sooner you answer them, the more practical and useful outreach promises will be to you.

1. Who are the pre-Christians (unbelievers) whom God has placed in my circle of family, friends, neighbors, and coworkers?
✏️

2. Who are the pre-Christians from ethnic groups different than my own whom God has placed within my community?
✏️

3. In what ways have I demonstrated Christ's love and shared His saving word with the people I listed in "1" and "2" above? ✎

4. For which missionaries, countries, peoples, or religions of the world has God given me a special concern? What have I done to support mission outreach among them? ✎

5. What joys of Christian outreach have I experienced? What obstacles are blocking my way? ✎

Prayer: Jesus, help me see and love those you place in my path.

Action: Review the five terms defined in the first half of this segment. Determine what your attitude is toward them.

C. Outreach Doubt

God loves us. That's good news! Even though God's loving plan is to announce His good news to others through people like you and me, sometimes we doubt if God knows what He's talking about. Satan tempted Eve with a question, "Did God really say...?" (Gen. 3:1). Similarly many Christians wonder, "Did God really mean it when He said all the world would hear of salvation in Christ?" The following vignettes, although fictional, describe the many forms outreach doubt takes around the globe.

United States of America. Dennis counts his church's offerings, about $3,000 for local use plus a few checks totaling $200 for evangelistic mission agencies. "What good will those gifts do?" he wonders. "Evangelizing the whole world is hopeless, isn't it? Six billion people. Hundreds of religions. Thousands of languages and cultures. It can't be done."

Dennis doubts God's plan to reach all peoples because of the magnitude of the task. What do you see of yourself in Dennis?
✏️

Canada. Clara sits in a chapel in Toronto. During the sermon, the preacher urges his flock to "go make disciples of all nations" (Mt. 28:19). Clara silently reflects: "Make disciples from all the nations? All the cultures? All the religions of the world? Jesus can't be serious! My neighbors here in Toronto are such a mixture of people. Jews. Arabs. Asians. Amerindians. They're so strange and difficult to understand, not merely their words but everything about them. Can we really witness to all the foreigners in this city—much less the world? I don't think it'll ever happen."

Clara doubts God's plan to reign in every culture, because cultures are so hard to relate to. What do you see of yourself in Clara? ✏️

Egypt. After Sunday worship, Sameh and Mina exit their church with its falling plaster and crippled furniture and walk home through the streets of Cairo, the intellectual center of Islam.

Sameh says to his friend, "Even though Muslims barely tolerate our presence in this city and do not allow us to keep our places of worship in good repair, my heart still aches for the nine million Muslims in Cairo. Mina, let's reach out to them."

"Why bother?" Mina scoffs. "We are Christians. They are Muslims. We don't trust them. They don't trust us. That's the way it has always been. That's how it always will be."

Mina refuses to believe the status quo can ever change. When have you thought witnessing to certain people was hopeless?
✏️

Place a ✔ where you stand on this scale.

outreach doubt |____|____|____|____|____| outreach trust

Good stings. Consider how the statements below move outreach doubters from inactivity to participation in God's mission.

___ A. Jesus commanded us to proclaim His gospel to the lost. If you truly love Him, you should obey Him all you can.

___ B. Because Christ forgives us and grants us eternal life, we ought to share the same blessings with others.

___ C. "People *will* come from east and west and north and south, and *will* take their places at the feast in the kingdom of God" (Lk. 13:29, emphasis mine).

"A" motivates with commands. It is true, but it stings. Ouch!

"B" is better than "A," because it motivates on the basis of the Gospel. However, due to its emphasis on "ought," it still stings when we fail to do God's will.

"C" promises what God will accomplish through us. It calls us from outreach doubt to outreach faith and is able to lead us from immobility to action. "C" is a good sting.

Prayer: Lord, what might happen to my outreach doubts if I learned to trust in your outreach promises?

Action: Share statements "A," "B," and "C" above with Christian friends. Which form of motivation appeals to them the most?

D. Outreach Fear

You love Jesus because He gladly gave His life for you. And yet your fears may prevent you from saying the name "Jesus" outloud. Outreach fear is familiar to Christians everywhere.

Germany. All the way home from work Gertrude scolded herself, "Here I've been praying for an open door to witness to Herr Lochner. When he began to tell about his friend's funeral, that was the opportunity. But then I fretted, 'He might become angry or laugh at me. Maybe he'll fire me.' Gertrude, you coward, your fears slammed the door God provided. And you did the same thing last year with Aunt Diedre. Hopeless! That's what you are."

What is the state of your confidence in regard to sharing your faith with others? 🖎

Uganda. Bakojja is a Christian in this East African country where one-third of the people have died of AIDS or developed its symptoms. Recently, the Holy Spirit has been tugging at Bakojja's heart to minister to AIDS victims. "Lord," he prays, "I've kept myself pure for you, and now you ask me to associate with sinners. What dangers for my soul. For my health too. This can't possibly be your will!"

What hazardous situations freeze you with outreach fear?

☞

Venezuela. Like many in Caracas, Marisela lives in a high-rise apartment building. Two months ago, her next-door neighbors Rómulo and Isabel were responding positively to her witness. Then one night while sitting on her balcony, Marisela overheard her downstairs neighbor chanting loudly, inviting three powerful spirit-gods to rule over the entire building and its occupants. Tobacco smoke used in the occult ritual drifted up and choked Marisela's apartment. After that night Rómulo and Isabel cooled toward the gospel. Now whenever Marisela thinks of witnessing to someone in her building, she shrugs "Why bother? The devil rules this turf."

How fearful are you about the spiritual warfare of evangelism?

☞

Place a ✔ where you stand on this scale.

outreach fear |____|____|____|____|____| outreach courage

Good stings. The Great Commission appears to be a foolhardy task until we notice its pre-promise and its post-promise. Here is the entire passage with the promises in italics.

"*All authority in heaven and on earth has been given to me.* Therefore go and make disciples of all nations, baptizing them in the name of the Father and of the Son and of the Holy Spirit, and teaching them to obey everything I have commanded you. *And surely I am with you always, to the very end of the age*" (Mt. 28:18-20).

How might Christ's promises about His universal authority and enduring presence transform outreach fear into outreach courage for Gertrude or Bakojja or Marisela or yourself? ✏️

Prayer: Father, help me exchange outreach fear for outreach courage by trusting in Your outreach promises.

Action: Ask others if they have outreach fears. Listen with care.

E. Outreach Discouragement

At times Christians overcome their outreach doubt and outreach fear. Some witness boldly. Some serve Christ in tough settings like inner cities and prisons. Some learn how to share Christ with people from other cultures. They labor. They serve. They love. They witness. But on occasion their determination ebbs, and they dwell in the shadow of outreach discouragement.

Thailand. At 6 AM Joyce sits in her Bangkok apartment. Other gray concrete apartment buildings tower nearby. Joyce writes on the cream-colored pages of her journal: "Lord, eight years ago, I longed to shine Your light in a dark place, and you graciously sent me here. I came not only to fulfill my dreams, but to fulfill Your dream that Thai Buddhists—and everyone everywhere—would hear the good news of Jesus Christ, so many might be saved. But so few have responded! Forgive my impatience, Lord, but is Your dream ever going to come true?"

When have the meager or slow results of your witnessing efforts discouraged you? ✏️

Ukraine. Pastor Zebrinski's radio rejoices, "Odessa wins the football match with a last minute goal!" Although Pastor Z.'s favorite team has won, he doesn't cheer. He's sound asleep stacking Zs. It's hard to cheer when you're exhausted. If he were awake, he'd tell you, "I work morning, noon, and night caring for four congregations. My soul would rejoice to see hundreds of converts added to my flock, but speaking honestly—and perhaps selfishly—I can't fathom having more sheep to tend. Even with the help of willing church members, I'm still overwhelmed. And now there's talk we Ukrainians should send missionaries to Muslim republics like Uzbekistan and Turkmenistan, where we are sure to meet with bitter opposition, even martyrdom. Pardon the pun, but I don't think I could 'istan' the extra work. It's hard to cheer when you're exhausted."

When have you or someone you know been exhausted for the sake of the gospel? ⇨

Place a ✔ where you stand on this scale.

outreach discouragement |___|___|___|___|___| outreach hope

Medicine for the mugged. We, the church, are like the traveler from Jerusalem to Jericho who fell among robbers in the parable of the Good Samaritan. En route to share Christ in our community or on distant shores, we have been mugged by outreach doubt, fear, and discouragement. Stripped of hope.

Wouldn't it be great if God, foreseeing we might lose heart, had promised us His global task could be and would be accomplished? HE DID! Just as the Good Samaritan poured oil and wine on the wounds of the beaten traveler, so God repeatedly promises that our witnessing and mission efforts will bear fruit.

The purpose of this book is to introduce you to the Bible's hundreds of outreach promises and teach you how to apply them to yourself and your church. Start with the good-sting verse below. Ponder it prayerfully. Apply it to your circumstances. How does it offer you healing for your personal outreach doubt, fear, and discouragement?

> For as the soil makes the sprout come up and a garden causes seeds to grow, so the Sovereign Lord will make righteousness and praise spring up before all nations (Is. 61:11).

Prayer: Holy Spirit, renew my hope to share the good news.

Action: Think of someone who might need outreach encouragement. Share with him or her the verse above.

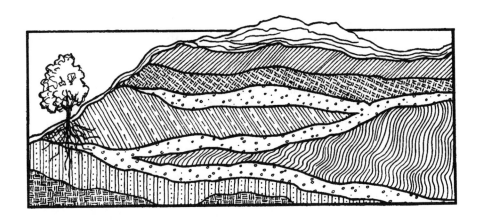

2 MINING A NEW VEIN OF PROPHECY

Christians treasure messianic prophecies, the Old Testament verses which point to the life and work of Jesus. Meanwhile, other precious prophecies lie overlooked, like a hidden gold mine.

A. The Vein of Messianic Prophecy

John Perling, a pastor in Beverly Hills, California, once told me an amazing story.

The phone rang six times before John realized it wasn't a dream. "Hello?" he mumbled.

A voice whispered, "Is this Pastor John Perling?"

"Uh huh. What time is it?"

"I'm Rabbi Isador Zwern from Temple of Aaron in Santa Monica. You don't know me, but could you please meet me for lunch at my home tomorrow?"

"I suppose," John yawned. He groped for a pencil and wrote down the address. "Rabbi, what's this all about?"

"Can't say more. Too risky. Tomorrow." Click.

John was used to predawn phone calls, but he'd never had one like this. So at noon he knocked on Rabbi Zwern's door and was greeted with a smile and an outstretched hand.

"Pastor, thank you for coming. Please forgive my treating you so secretively last night. I couldn't afford to have my family overhear. They're all out of the house right now."

Rabbi Zwern invited John into the dining room. Amid the tableware and food lay his large Hebrew Bible placed as though it were to be part of the meal. They began to eat while engaging in getting-acquainted conversation. Over matzo ball soup, the Rabbi opened his Bible and began to reveal his mystery.

"I've been studying the Holy Scriptures of Isaiah and other prophets. What astonishing discoveries I've made! For example, Isaiah 53:4-5 says:

> Surely he took up our infirmities and carried our sorrows, yet we considered him stricken by God, smitten by him, and afflicted. But he was pierced for our transgressions, he was crushed for our iniquities; the punishment that brought us peace was upon him, and by his wounds we are healed.

"Pastor, do you know about whom Isaiah is speaking?"

John certainly did. But before he could answer, the rabbi said, "I think it refers to Jesus of Nazareth. Surely He fulfilled these words of the prophet."

"I think you've got something there."

Eyes sparkling with delight, Rabbi Zwern raced from one prophecy to another and repeated, "Do you know whom the prophet is talking about?" And every time he voiced his new-found faith: "I think the prophet is speaking about Jesus of Nazareth. He must be the Promised Messiah."

The two men continued to eat, but food was hardly needed. The Word of God was the main course at this meal.

Today Isador Zwern still confesses "*Yeshua ha Meshiach,* Jesus the Messiah!" His story is not unique. The messianic prophecies, which foretold events centuries before their occurrence, are one of the greatest proofs of the Christian faith. Through the centuries, they have persuaded the minds and hearts of many skeptics.

When pre-Christians tell you, "I'd believe in God if He would perform a miracle right before my eyes," you can open your Bible and declare, "Here, feast your eyes on a whole flock of miracles. They are called messianic prophecies."

Think mining. Picture the Bible as a mountain. Running through it is a vein of literature called messianic prophecy. All the promises foretelling Christ's life and His work of redemption are like a bonanza of gold and jewels. Just as geologists and miners dig treasures out of the earth, so Christians delve into the Bible to find messianic promises which lead us to trust in Christ.

Which details of Christ's life, foretold in messianic prophecies, have been most significant to you? ◎⇨

Nothing could match the messianic prophecies. Nothing. Unless... unless somehow more treasures still lay undiscovered. If a whole vein of promises from God lay overlooked and unexploited, would you dig in and explore it?

Prayer: Holy Spirit, thank You for the miracle of prophecies.
Action: Read Isaiah 53 and marvel at the details foretold there.

B. The Vein of Outreach Prophecy

Luke tells us that on Easter evening, Jesus "opened their minds so they could understand the Scriptures." Do you want to understand too? Listen. He said: "Everything must be fulfilled that is written about me in the Law of Moses, the Prophets and the Psalms.... This is what is written: The Christ will suffer and rise from the dead on the third day,..." (Lk. 24:44, 46).

The Risen Savior wants to open our minds to the many messianic promises which He, the Messiah, fulfilled.

A discovery. But wait a minute! In Jesus' words quoted above, we read only half of what the Lord said to open our minds to understand the Scriptures. Look at the entire sentence in Luke 24:46-47, arranged in verse form:

"This is what is written:
The Christ will suffer and rise again on the third day,
and
repentance and forgiveness of sins will be preached
in his name to all nations, beginning at Jerusalem."

In the last two lines, Jesus refers to prophecies about believers extending His invitation of salvation to all nations. What have we stumbled upon here? Could Jesus be pointing to another category of prophecy in the Bible? Yes. That is exactly what He is doing. In addition to the messianic prophecies, He speaks of another vein of prophecies in Scripture, outreach prophecies. They promise God will empower us to herald the gospel both to our neighbors and to distant nations. (Other allusions to outreach prophecy appear in: Acts 3:21-26; 10:43; 26:22-23; 2 Cor. 4:5; Eph. 1:9-10; 3:8-9; 1 Pet. 1:11; Rev. 5:9-10.)

A game. Let's play the Psalm 22 Game. Although David composed this psalm centuries before the invention of crucifixion, it describes the sufferings of Christ in detail. Write down verses or ideas you recall from Psalm 22. ◉⇨

Did you remember verse 1, "My God, my God, why have you forsaken me?" Verses 7-8 describe the mocking of His accusers. Verse 14 portrays His agonized suffering. Verse 15 tells why Jesus requested a drink. Details of the crucifixion and the soldiers gambling for Jesus' clothes are foretold in verses 16-18.

Wow! These are 24-carat messianic prophecies.

You probably did pretty well with this game. Or at least the verses sounded familiar when I mentioned them.

Second half. The game is not over. All the verses mentioned above are from the first eighteen verses of Psalm 22. What verses or ideas do you recall from the rest of the psalm? ◉⇨

Are you curious how Psalm 22 ends? Verses 27-31 contain marvelous predictions.

All the ends of the earth will remember and turn to the LORD, and all the families of the nations will bow down before him, for dominion belongs to the LORD and he rules over the nations. All the rich of the earth will feast and worship; all who go down to the dust will kneel before him—those who cannot keep themselves alive. Posterity will serve him; future generations will be told about the Lord. They will proclaim his righteousness to a people yet unborn—for he has done it.

Key phrases from Psalm 22 show us that the promised Savior will impact all the world. No one is omitted.
- Geographic: "all the ends of the earth"
- Political: "the nations"
- Ethnic: "all the families of the nations"
- Socioeconomic: "all the rich… all who go down to the dust"
- Chronological: "future generations… people yet unborn"

Lessons. Playing the Psalm 22 Game taught us two lessons. First, messianic prophecies and outreach prophecies often appear together. Second, if we lack a mental category labeled "outreach prophecies," we will tend to overlook them.

The Lord wants us to mine both veins of prophecy for the distinct treasures found in each.

Prayer: Christ, open my mind to understand the Scriptures by showing me the treasures in the vein of outreach prophecy.

Action: Invite someone else to play the Psalm 22 Game.

C. The Honor of Fulfilling Outreach Prophecy

A question. Jesus the Messiah, fulfills the messianic prophecies which foretell events of His life and ministry. But who fulfills the outreach prophecies?

Consider these words spoken by Peter the Missionary before the Jewish supreme council. "God exalted him [Jesus] to his own right hand as Prince and Savior that he might give repentance and forgiveness of sins to Israel. *We* are witnesses of these things, and so is *the Holy Spirit…*" (Acts 5:31-32, emphasis mine). According to Peter, witnessing the gospel to lost people is an honor shared by the Holy Spirit and by people who confess Christ.

An honor. When you share Christ with a friend, you are fulfilling evangelism prophecy. When you write a missionary an encouraging letter, you are fulfilling mission prophecy. Even though no Bible verse states specifically, "In the future, on this exact date, you will do such and such," your witnessing efforts are implied and included in outreach prophecies such as: "My name will be great among the nations, from the rising to the setting of the sun" (Mal. 1:11); and "...you shine like stars in the universe as you hold out the word of life..." (Phil. 2:15-16).

Through your witness and mission activity, you have the honor of participating in the fulfillment of outreach prophecy. How does this make you feel? ☞

Ongoing prophecies. I nominate the Energizer® Bunny as a Christian symbol. This pink, mechanical rabbit is the corporate symbol of a battery manufacturer. The advertisements claim his long-lasting batteries keep him going and going. So why nominate the Energizer® Bunny as a Christian symbol? Let me explain.

When we celebrate the coming of the Magi to worship the Christ child, we often read this prophecy from Psalm 72:10: "The kings of Sheba and Seba will present him gifts." On the basis of this verse, many a preacher has concluded, "When the Magi presented gold, incense, and myrrh to Jesus, the prophecy of Psalm 72 was fulfilled."

I agree. And I disagree. When the Magi came, the prophecy was not *completely* fulfilled, rather it *began* to be fulfilled. Many outreach promises, including this one, keep on going and going, just like the Energizer® Bunny.

Psalm 72 was written either *by* King Solomon or *for* him. In either case, it predicts the coming of a king who will establish universal peace and justice. The psalm abounds with expressions like: "For he will deliver the needy who cry out, the afflicted who have no one to help" (v. 12). In addition, the psalm describes the king's reign as ongoing and global.

> He will rule from sea to sea and from the River [Euphrates] to the ends of the earth. The desert tribes will bow before him and his enemies will lick the dust. The Kings of Tarshish [Spain] and of distant shores will bring tribute to him; the kings of Sheba and Seba [southwest Arabia] will present him gifts. All kings will bow down to him and all nations will serve him.... May his name endure forever; may it continue as long as the sun. All nations will be blessed through him, and they will call him blessed (8-11, 17).

The kings of Israel could never fulfill these messianic/outreach prophecies, because they were mortal, finite, and prone to sin. Only an eternal, all-powerful, and holy King can work these wonders. Only Jesus of Nazareth, King of the Jews, can fulfill the prophecy. He began to do so when the Magi visited Him, and He continues to do so today through the evangelistic expansion of His reign. Whenever rulers and other power brokers trust in Christ as their Savior, Psalm 72 is still being fulfilled. Whenever, in the name of Christ the King, believers serve the needy and rescue them from oppression, Psalm 72 is still being fulfilled.

To participate with the Holy Spirit in the fulfillment of such prophecies is the highest joy and honor. May God's ongoing outreach prophecies energize you to keep on going and going and going: in prayer, in serving those in need, in witnessing, and in church planting at home and abroad.

Now can you picture the Energizer® Bunny in a stained-glass window?

Prayer: Jesus, I praise You for the honor of proclaiming You.

Action: Since outreach prophecies are ongoing, what outreach activity do you think God has planned for you to do today?

D. The Vein of End Times Prophecy

When you study outreach prophecies, you also are likely to encounter prophecies dealing with the end of earth's history and the return of Christ. Look how the Lord links all three kinds of prophecy in Matthew 24:14: "And this gospel of the kingdom [messianic prophecy] will be preached in the whole world as a testimony to all nations [outreach prophecy], and then the end will come [end times prophecy]."

Exactly when the task of world evangelization will be completed is difficult to determine. Our definitions of the key terms in this verse (preach, testimony, and nations) may vary. What matters most is how the Lord defines them. We should stick to our task until we reach the level of evangelizing the world which He considers sufficient, "and then the end will come" (Mt. 24:14).

Three veins. The Bible is like a mountain with three veins of prophecy in it. One vein is messianic prophecy, describing what Christ would do when He came to live on earth two thousand years ago. A second vein is end times prophecy, describing the last days and what Christ will do when He returns. Because Bible scholars have excavated both of these veins extensively, we know a lot about both messianic prophecies and end times prophecies. Hundreds of scholars have written books on them. Thousands of artists and musicians have created works based on them. Millions of sermons have been preached about them.

Meanwhile, in between these two veins of prophecy lies a third—the vein of outreach prophecies. Are hundreds of books written about them? Are thousands of works of art and millions of sermons based on outreach prophecies? No. We have only scratched the surface of this vein. The purpose of this book is to help us all start digging.

Setting dates. Some Christians use end times prophecies to calculate the time when Christ will return. In the same way, some may attempt to use outreach prophecies to compute a date when the Great Commission will be completed and the end will come. But the Bible doesn't tell us an exact When. "No one knows about that day or hour..." (Mk. 13:32). Outreach prophecies do, however, tell us we are to:

- What? Proclaim Christ.
- To whom? To every person.
- Where? In every place.
- How? By the Holy Spirit's power.
- Why? Because God loves them.

The When that matters the most is right Now. God has placed you and me on the earth Now, so we each can play our one-person-sized roles in completing His mission.

Think of Europe's medieval cathedrals, which took generations of builders to complete. Some dug the foundations. Some laid the stones. Others crafted the interior carpentry. The artisan who laid the last pane of stained glass was not superior to the laborer who dug the first ditch for the foundation. All who participated in the massive enterprise were Cathedral Builders, contributing what they had to offer in the Now in which God placed them.

Similarly, evangelizing the world requires generations of builders. Some witness to family and friends. Some care for the homeless or oppressed. Others are missionaries in distant places. The persons who will witness to Christ on the final day of history will not be superior to those who shared their faith in earlier times. Whatever you and I contribute in our Now is an essential step toward the ultimate fulfillment of outreach prophecy.

Prayer: Lord of the Ages, thank You for this present Now in which I play my one-person-sized role to expand Your Kingdom.

Action: Think of the patience and perseverance required for cathedral construction. How is it like building God's Kingdom?

E. Outreach Prophecy and the Millennium

Multiple opinions. Unfortunately, Christians disagree regarding end times prophecy and, in particular, regarding the millennium. This is the teaching in Revelation 20 that Christ will reign on the earth for a thousand years. Here are brief descriptions of the most common views regarding the timing and nature of the millennium. Which view do you hold? Do you have an opinion?

- Amillennialism: the millennium is this present age in which Christ reigns in the lives of believers and expands His kingdom daily as the gospel is proclaimed.
- Postmillennialism: the millennium will be a literal "golden age" on earth, or it will symbolize the final triumph of the gospel, after which Christ will return.
- Premillennialism: at Christ's return, believers will reign on earth with Christ for one thousand years. After that time, Satan will lead a rebellion, culminating in his complete defeat. (To explain the distinctive differences between historic premillennialism and dispensational premillennialism is beyond the scope of this book.)

I wish to be honest with you and let you know I am an amillennialist. However, to learn about outreach promises, you don't need to understand all the views concerning the millennium, nor do you need to agree with my position. I have broached the subject, because disagreements about the millennium may cause us to overlook outreach prophecies and the promises contained in them.

When an amillennialist reads a text with elements of both outreach prophecy and end times prophecy, he or she may think, "This makes me feel uncomfortable, because it sounds like an earthly millennial reign. I'd better skim over these verses."

Similarly, when a postmillennialist or a premillennialist reads such a text, he or she may conclude, "I think this speaks about a future age in history. So I guess it has little or nothing to say to me today."

In both cases, the outreach lessons in the text are ignored.

A mountain devotion. In 1997, I led devotions for a Missionary Family Retreat in Venezuela. One day we rode a cable car up into the Andes mountains. At that high elevation, I led a devotion on Isaiah 2:2-4. You can experience this devotion right now. Picture yourself seated amid the beautiful tundra flowers on the slopes of the Andes. A vast panorama lies before you.

1. How does being in the mountains change your perspective?
2. Which is the most important mountain in the Bible? Why?
3. Here is how the Lord answers the previous question:

In the last days the mountain of the Lord's temple will be established as chief among the mountains; it will be raised above the hills, and all nations will stream to it.

Many peoples will come and say, "Come, let us go up to the mountain of the LORD, to the house of the God of Jacob. He will teach us his ways, so that we may walk in his paths." The law will go out from Zion, the word of the LORD from Jerusalem. He will judge between the nations and will settle disputes for many peoples. They will beat their swords into plowshares and their spears into pruning hooks. Nation will not take up sword against nation, nor will they train for war anymore (Is. 2:2-4).

4. Isaiah 2:2-4 is an outreach prophecy. What does it tell us about the mission of God? In what ways has this prophecy been fulfilled in Latin America? In what ways does it still await fulfillment? What details of the text give you hope for the future?
5. The Andes mountain range, where we now stand, is the backbone of South America. I invite you to use your imagination. Picture yourself as a giant condor slowly flying the length of the Andes. From Venezuela and Colombia in the north, through

Ecuador, Peru, Bolivia, Chile and Argentina. About five thousand miles!

6. As you fly, notice the many villages and cities found here. The peoples, languages, and customs. Also the many false gods and deceiving spirits which far too many people serve.

7. Now, from your condor perspective picture all the Christians who live here. See their churches, their worship and songs, their communities of faith and hope in Christ, their works of love, and their words which testify to the gospel. See the miracle of people delivered out of slavery to false gods into saving faith in Christ. See the word of God settling disputes where injustice previously reigned. See peace growing between nations, ethnic groups, and economic classes.

8. This vision of Christian work in Latin America is not our own idea. It is foreshadowed in the words of God in Isaiah 2:2-4.

Write down any interesting details the Lord showed you during your imagined flight through the Andes. ▱

A pickax. I hope this treatment of Isaiah 2:2-4 has shown you that, while I am an amillennialist, I am not writing to grind a millennial ax. Instead, I'm fashioning a trusty, outreach pickax to help you mine the Bible's vein of outreach prophecy. Christians of all millennial viewpoints can and should dig into the vein of outreach prophecy. Even though our interpretations of some texts will differ greatly, we can all gain encouragement to share our faith from the outreach promises found in God's Word.

In the next chapter we will investigate the precious materials the Lord has placed in the vein of outreach prophecy. What could be more fun than digging for treasure?

Prayer: Lord, even though we interpret the Scriptures in different ways, thank You for the encouragement of outreach prophecies.

Action: Regardless of your millennial position, identify a promise in Isaiah 2:2-4 which helps you share Christ in your Now.

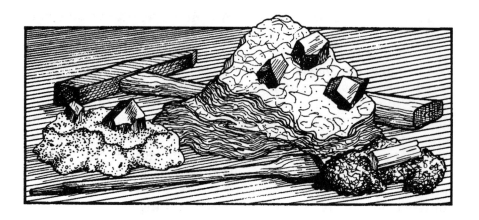

3 *MATERIALS IN THE VEIN OF OUTREACH PROPHECY*

In the vein of outreach prophecy, we find different materials. Each has its own purpose and value, but the most precious—like glittering gems—are outreach promises.

A. Outreach Commands and Warnings

Mining can be dark, dirty, and dangerous. While you read the next few pages, the earth will tremble and you'll expect a cave-in. But fear not. God has lessons for you to learn even in the dark.

Outreach commands. The vein of outreach prophecy contains many commands to spread Christ's gospel. Here are two.

Sing to the LORD, praise his name; proclaim his salvation day after day. Declare his glory among the nations, his marvelous deeds among all peoples (Ps. 96:2-3).

He said to them, "Go into all the world and preach the good news to all creation" (Mk. 16:15).

Outreach Warnings. The vein of outreach prophecy also contains warnings to people who fail to witness as God desires.

The Lord promised the patriarch Jacob, "Your descendants will be like the dust of the earth, and you will spread out to the west and to the east, to the north and to the south. All peoples on earth will be blessed through you and your offspring"

(Gen. 28:14). Ultimately, the Jews would bless all nations when Jesus the Jewish Messiah came to redeem us all. In addition, God wanted the righteous conduct of every Jew to draw others to faith in Him.

Often, however, Israel's unfaithfulness and idolatry led the nations away from God. After they were conquered and exiled, the Lord declared, "Israel is swallowed up, now she is among the nations like a worthless thing" (Hos. 8:8).

Similar warnings of judgment are in the New Testament. Paul laments, "God's name is blasphemed among the nations because of you" (Rom. 2:24). Jesus said, "But he who disowns me before men will be disowned before the angels of God" (Lk. 12:9).

Their purpose. Why did God place outreach commands and outreach warnings in the Bible? Outreach commands reveal God's desire to save all people and His plan to use us as His ambassadors to the lost. Outreach warnings alert us to the danger of selfishly keeping God's blessings to ourselves. We need this information to counteract Satan's sugar-coated counsel:

> Christians do not need to proclaim the gospel of Christ to non-Christians, because God surely will pardon all good, sincere people regardless of what religion they follow.

What do you think of this idea? What do God's outreach commands and warnings teach you about its truth value?

Inner accusations. Like heartburn after pepperoni pizza, talking about outreach commands and warnings can result in a guilty conscience. Place a ✔ by the accusations you have felt.

__ a. I don't know if I can rise to these challenges.
__ b. At times I've failed to witness when I should have.
__ c. So much needs to be done, and I'm only one person.
__ d. I feel pressured to witness to everyone I meet.
__ e. I am weighed down by the lost state of billions of people.
__ f. I feel guilty for not having done more in the past.
__ g. I don't love people enough to sacrifice for their sake.

Don't feel bad if you check all seven. I could. God's outreach commands and warnings accuse us, simply because we are imperfect witnesses. Sometimes we are just plain lazy or cowardly or apathetic about the people who face eternity without Christ.

Reinforce the ceiling. At this point you might be thinking: "Thanks a heap for dragging me into this mine. I suspected this topic might arouse guilt feelings, and now it has. When I hear God's law in His outreach commands and warnings, I feel tremors of judgment about to bring the ceiling tumbling down on us."

We need some solid timbers to reinforce our mine. You will find those timbers in the next section.

Prayer: Lord, keep me safe as I venture into this mine.

Action: Recall an experience in which the Bible's outreach commands and warnings made you quake with guilt.

B. Braced by Grace

God designed outreach commands and warnings to show us our failure to be a light to the nations, so that we might repent of our disobedience and apathy. However, all by themselves, outreach commands and warnings can not motivate or empower us to perform what they require. So, when we are flattened by a cave-in of guilt and shame, what can we do?

Gospel promises. We do what Christians always do with their sins. We confess our faults and lean on God's mercy toward us, His mediocre ambassadors. Read the four gospel promises below and feel the rubble of sin and shame lifted off you. For emphasis, I took the liberty to add brief comments in brackets.

1. [God] has saved us and called us to a holy life—not because of anything we have done [such as evangelizing the lost] but because of his own purpose and grace. This grace was given us in Christ Jesus... (2 Tim. 1:9).

2. But if anyone does sin [against God's command to make disciples], we have one who speaks to the Father in our defense—Jesus Christ, the Righteous One. He is the atoning sacrifice for our sins, and not only for ours but also for the sins of the whole world (1 Jn. 2:1-2).

3. For it is by grace [not by evangelistic activity] you have been saved, through faith—and this not from your-

selves, it is the gift of God—not by works [even diligent mission works], so that no one can boast (Eph. 2:8-9).

4. Then they asked him, "What must we do to do the works God requires?" Jesus answered, "The work of God is this: to believe in the one he has sent [plus nothing]" (Jn. 6:28-29).

Which statement best summarizes these gospel promises?

__ a. I am saved by doing my best to evangelize the world.

__ b. I am saved by trusting only in the saving work of Christ.

For those who believe the gospel, the answer is obvious, but we must tell our accusing consciences the truth repeatedly, so that we always rest on the Lord and not on our own efforts.

Sturdy beams. Exploring the vein of outreach prophecy can be scary. Without strong timbers to brace the walls and ceiling, we would perish in a cave-in of guilt. But our gracious Lord has provided sturdy timbers for our safety—the very beams of the cross of Christ. We are safe, because of God's solid, enduring promises to give us redemption, pardon, peace, and eternal life.

With this security, we can continue to mine the vein of outreach prophecy without fear.

Prayer: Lord, in the blood of Jesus, cleanse me of my outreach failures, as You faithfully do with all my other sins.

Action: Recall an experience in which a gospel promise comforted you and assured you that your faith is worth sharing.

C. Outreach Promises

Good, the tremors are over. Now we are safe to proceed digging. So far, we have excavated outreach commands and warnings. While they are useful, God deposited something else—something glittering and precious—in the vein of outreach prophecy. Keep digging. We are about to unearth God's good stings for Christian outreach.

Mixing metaphors. An English teacher would have slashed the previous sentence with a red pencil. I mixed two metaphors, combined two different word pictures. This is a literary no-no. But I did it on purpose. Outreach promises are so grand that one metaphor alone can not do them justice. Throughout this book I use two word pictures.

First, outreach promises are like gems concealed in the earth of the Bible. To mine them takes effort, but you will be amazed at their value and usefulness. Second, outreach promises are good stings, God's cure for the outreach paralysis caused by doubt, fear, and discouragement. A regular dose of this medicine will invigorate you to share Christ near and far.

Rather than mixing metaphors, I prefer to think of this as constructing with two good materials, like stones and mortar.

Outreach hope. In Romans 15 Paul the Missionary reveals his skill as a prospector of outreach promises. Let's begin with Romans 15:4: "Everything that was written in the past was written to teach us, so that through endurance and the encouragement of the Scriptures we might have hope."

What kind of hope is Paul talking about? In the Bible "hope" often refers to the hope of heaven, but the context reveals this is not the case here. In Romans 13-14 Paul urges mutual acceptance in mission churches which were experiencing intercultural tensions. In the second half of Romans 15, he invites the Christians in Rome to participate in a missionary expedition to Spain. The context reveals that the hope in Romans 15:4 is not the hope of heaven, but the hope of evangelizing the nations.

Outreach hope!

To motivate the Romans to support the mission to Spain, Paul could have resorted to outreach commands or warnings, but he knew endurance and encouragement arise from outreach promises, not outreach commands or warnings. That's why he refers to outreach promises in Romans 15:8: "For I tell you that Christ has become a servant of the Jews on behalf of God's truth, *to confirm the promises made to the patriarchs*" (italics mine).

Some may argue that the phrase in italics only refers to messianic promises. However, Paul surely is also referring to outreach promises, because he continues by quoting four of them:

> ... so that the Gentiles may glorify God for his mercy as it is written: "Therefore I will praise you among the Gentiles; I will sing hymns to your name" [2 Sam. 22:50]. Again, it says, "Rejoice, O Gentiles, with his people" [Dt. 32:43]. And again, "Praise the Lord, all you Gentiles, and sing praises to him, all you peoples" [Ps. 117:1].

And again Isaiah says, "The Root of Jesse [Christ] will spring up, one who will arise to rule over the nations; the Gentiles will hope in him" [Is. 11:10] (Rom. 15:9-12).

Outreach promises. Paul reaches into the vein of outreach prophecy and pulls out four gems glistening with hope. Some outreach promises are like "the Gentiles will hope in him." They are prophecies stated in the future tense concerning the spread of the gospel. Other outreach promises are like "sing praises to him, all you peoples" or "I will praise you among the Gentiles." These don't sound like promises, but Paul, Missionary to the Gentiles, understood them as statements of optimism that God will fulfill His global purposes. All four verses are good stings.

Since Paul defines outreach promises so broadly, so should we. An outreach promise is any word God has given us, "so that through endurance and the encouragement of the Scriptures we might have hope" to proclaim the name of Christ (Rom. 15:4).

When we know and rely on God's outreach promises, we are more likely to obey His outreach commands. The promises assure us He will bless our efforts to expand His kingdom of grace to others.

Outreach prophecy. Before we go on, I should clarify that I use the term "outreach prophecy" in two ways.

In the *wide* sense, the word "prophecy" means anything said or written by a prophet or other biblical author. Therefore, outreach prophecy in the wide sense is any Bible text which talks about expanding God's kingdom by proclaiming the gospel. All such outreach prophecy in the wide sense is the source of what Bible scholars call the biblical theology of evangelism and mission. I have been using this wide definition when I refer to the vein of outreach prophecy.

In a *narrow* sense, outreach prophecy refers to the predictions of global evangelism mentioned by Jesus in Luke 24:47. An example is Isaiah 11:10, quoted by Paul in Romans 15:12 above. An outreach prophecy in the narrow sense is always an outreach promise as well. Whenever I speak of outreach prophecies in the plural, I am talking about predictions like these.

Prayer: Holy Spirit, replace my outreach pessimism with hope.
Action: To get the big picture of Romans 15, read the entire chapter.

Group

D. Appraising Outreach Promises

A gemologist uses several criteria to appraise the value of precious stones: color, hardness, size, purity, and so on.

No matter how you look at outreach promises, they are invaluable. Here are several reasons to learn outreach promises and use them. Ponder the significance of each factor.

1. In the same way that gospel promises contain the power to produce faith in Christ and save you, so God's outreach promises create faith that God will carry out His mission through you.

2. "Promise" and "missionary" come from the Latin word *mittere*, meaning "to send." A missionary is one who is sent. A promise is a message that is sent forth. God won't send you ten feet or ten thousand miles without promises to sustain you.

3. Since God is faithful to His promises, you have the right to claim outreach promises and pray for what they offer.

4. You aren't trapped at your present level of witnessing skill. Outreach promises are solid ground for expectations of growth.

5. God's mission is not stuck at its present stage of expansion. Despite obstacles and setbacks, God promises ongoing advances.

6. Aristotle said, "A vivid imagination compels the whole body to obey it." When we tune in to outreach promises, God's vivid imagination compels the Body of Christ to act.

7. Business literature advises company executives to cast a vision of what they want their companies to become. God has practiced this all along, casting His vision so you will see and accept your personal role in His global mission of mercy.

8. George Santayana said, "Those who do not remember the past are condemned to relive it." Likewise, Christians who don't remember the future may miss out on it. How can you remember the future? In outreach promises God describes the future growth of His church and calls you to participate in it.

9. You don't have to feel like an uncoordinated kid waving anxiously hoping God will choose you to play on His team. The Lord hasn't reluctantly picked you last. From the beginning of time, He chose you for His outreach team.

10. Like snowflakes and fingerprints, each outreach promise is distinctly different, because the Holy Spirit gave each promise

in a unique historical context. Also, the insights you and I gain from a particular outreach promise vary according to the unique situations in which God places us as His witnesses. We will see many examples of this in coming chapters.

Which of the ten reasons struck you as significant? Why?

Summary. Outreach commands and warnings serve a good purpose. They point us to God's will that we be His witnesses. However, since we often fall short of His will, these texts can also accuse us. Thank God, confidence in His gospel frees us from bearing this load.

Outreach promises serve a higher purpose. They are God's good stings to empower us to serve pre-Christians with Christlike love and announce His mercy to them.

Prayer: Lord, help me see the future with Your outreach vision.

Action: Made bold by God's outreach promises, reach out today to someone you know who needs Christ.

E. Prospecting 101

To discover jewels, you must be able to distinguish gems from mere stones. To mine outreach promises, you need to know what you are looking for.

Familiar verses. One of the best places to find *outreach* promises is in *gospel* promises. Consider the classic text John 3:16. "For God so loved the world that he gave his one and only Son, that whoever believes in him shall not perish but have eternal life." This verse brims with encouraging phrases for us who believe this gospel promise and wish to proclaim it to others.

"The world" shows the good news is for all with whom you ever share it. You are never wasting your breath.

"Whoever believes" affirms that miraculous conversions surely will occur by the Holy Spirit's working.

"Shall not perish" points to the eternal success of the rescue operation performed by witnessing about your Savior.

Less familiar. Here is a lesser known gospel promise. "On this mountain he will destroy the shroud that enfolds all peoples, the sheet that covers all nations; he will swallow up death forever. The Sovereign LORD will wipe away the tears from all faces..." (Is. 25:7-8). The phrase "on this mountain" points us to Calvary where, for a time, it seemed death had gobbled Jesus up. But in reality He had swallowed up death—forever.

Outreach encouragement abounds in the phrases "all peoples," "all nations," and "from all faces." Where Christ is not known, death is a riddle. Hard-boiled agnostics in the West admit they don't have the answer to the riddle of death. Hindus spreading the ashes of their dead on the Ganges River do not know the answer. Nor do animistic Africans who serve—and at times fear—the spirits of departed ancestors. But in Isaiah 25:7-8, God vows that announcing Christ's resurrection to your neighbors and to the nations will indeed solve the riddle for those who hear and believe.

All-inclusive. John 3:16 and Isaiah 25:7-8, quoted above, are rich in all-inclusive terms like "all," "world," "nations," "peoples," and "whoever." When you hear your pickax clink against an all-inclusive term, you are probably near an outreach promise. Circle the all-inclusive terms in the verses below.

...the son of Man did not come to be served, but to serve, and to give his life as a ransom for many (Mt. 20:28).

But I, when I am lifted up from the earth, will draw all men to myself (Jn. 12:32; see Is. 11:10.).

This is not a mere word-search exercise. It's people-search too. As you read these all-inclusive terms, what pre-Christian friends or unevangelized people groups come to mind?

Subtle promises. Outreach promises can also be subtle. John 14:6 is an example: "I am the way and the truth and the life. No one comes to the Father except through me."

At first glance, this may not appear to be an outreach promise. But think about it. The words "way," "truth," and "life" are often used to describe religions. If you take this into account, Jesus is saying, "No human religion can grant people salvation. But I surely can!" This promise should renew our determination to witness to people who claim all religions are the same.

Bible stories. Not all outreach promises are brief statements. Entire Bible stories also can be considered outreach promises.

For example, the story of God healing Naaman the leper in 2 Kings 5 reveals how the Lord desires to save people who do not yet know Him. Jesus even referred to this story in His first sermon in Nazareth as an example of how He intended to proclaim the kingdom of God (Lk. 4:16-27).

In John 3 we find Jesus speaking about conversion to Nicodemus, a pious, wealthy and influential Jewish man. In the next chapter, John 4, Jesus talks about living water to a loose-living, poor and unimportant Samaritan woman. These two people could hardly be more opposite. Yet they both need the same thing, the grace of God in Jesus Christ. God can call anyone to faith, regardless of where he or she may stand on the wide continuum between Nicodemus and the woman at the well.

Bible stories such as these are outreach promises. At the same time, individual verses within the stories can also be outreach promises. See Jn. 3:17-18 and 4:35-38 for examples.

An invitation. Outreach promises are the precious gems in the vein of outreach prophecy. So put on your miner's helmet, grab your pick, and let's go digging for outreach promises.

If you were touring a diamond mine, the guide would warn you, "No samples allowed! You can look, but you can't touch!"

However, this mine belongs to God, and He placed these gems in it to help you overcome your outreach doubts, fears, and discouragement. So, in the coming chapters when you see something interesting, go ahead and grab it. Hold it up to the light. Turn it in your hand. Enjoy its beauty. Keep it. It's yours.

Prayer: Lord, I never realized you offered me such riches! Help me to identify Your outreach promises and treasure them.

Action: On a card write an outreach promise from this chapter. Commit it to memory, and repeat it for personal encouragement.

4 OUTREACH PROMISES AND SHARING YOUR FAITH

In this chapter we will consider several outreach promises which motivate you to witness about your Savior. There are many more where these came from. "Ooh! Aah!" you'll exclaim as you continually find outreach promises in your own Bible reading.

A. Focus on the Right "I"

The wrong "I". The biggest obstacle many of us face is our own distrust of our ability to witness well. Sharing our faith with a friend or family member is difficult. Our anxieties are multiplied when we consider reaching out to someone quite different from us, such as a Muslim, a Buddhist, a New Age adherent, or a drug addict.

How many of the following apprehensions have made you hesitate to share your faith?

__ I'm not sure what to say. What if I say it wrong?
__ I might not be able to answer the questions people ask me.
__ I might offend them and turn them off to the gospel forever.

Circle the only pronoun which occurs in all three of the above apprehensions. Perhaps you are focusing on the wrong "I."

The right "I." When Jesus called His disciples, they were novices, unprepared to proclaim His salvation to the world. So Jesus promised them, "Come, follow me, and I will make you fishers of men" (Mt. 4:19). This verse is so familiar we often skim over the wonderful promise found in it. Jesus points to His long-term goal to make His disciples fishers of lost people. To fulfill His promise, the Lord trained the first disciples for three years.

Those disciples had a lot to learn. So do you. According to Matthew 4:19, if you follow Jesus, His training will progress steadily until the goal is reached. You *will* become a fisher of men. Take personal inventory. To more effectively love pre-Christians and share your faith, what knowledge, attitudes, and skills do you need to acquire? ▭▷

If you focus on the wrong "I," namely yourself, you are likely to doubt you will become a fisher of men. But look at the promise again. "Come, follow, me," Jesus said, "and I will make you fishers of men." Who is the "I" in this verse? Not you, but Jesus! With you as the apprentice and Jesus as the teacher, what is the likelihood He can make you exactly what He promises, a fisher of the lost? Surely He can do it. In prayer ask Him to begin the process today. Jesus will use three methods to teach you.

Modeling. Jesus teaches by example. He said, "As the Father has sent me, I am sending you" (Jn. 20:21). The word "as" is crucial. The Father sent His Son as an evangelistic missionary. Jesus promises that as He did, so we can do. As He loved, so we can love. As He served, so we can serve. As He spoke, so we can speak. In every Bible story about Jesus, you will find Him modeling for you how to love, serve, and speak.

Team. Christ teaches you and others. In Luke 10 Jesus sent out seventy-two disciples two by two. Paul followed the same principle by always traveling in a team. When Jesus promised, "I will make you fishers of men," the word "you" is plural. Evangelism works best as a group activity, rather than an individual one.

What differences will occur when you "play the game" of Christian outreach as a team? Who would you like to have on your team? ▭▷

Trainers. The Lord also teaches through pastors and other mature leaders. Paul advises Timothy, "And the things you have heard me say in the presence of many witnesses entrust to reliable men who will also be qualified to teach others" (2 Tim. 2:2). The chain of training—from Jesus, to Paul, to Timothy, to reliable men, to others—has never been broken. So link up and learn.

Who are the evangelism and mission teachers God has provided for you? ✏️▷

Focus on the right "I," Jesus, and you will find Him transforming you into something you always longed to be—but perhaps doubted was possible—a fisher of lost people.

Prayer: Jesus, You are making me a fisher of people. Help me to see the process and rejoice in the progress.

Action: Identify a few Christians with whom you would enjoy doing outreach. Talk to them about sharing your faith as a team.

B. So-Called Hopeless Cases

When it comes to Christian outreach, many folks feel like giving up hope. However, you and your church are not hopeless cases. Neither are the people to whom you witness.

So-called hopeless churches. In Philippians 1:6, Paul says, "He who began a good work in you will carry it on to completion until the day of Christ Jesus." How do you understand this promise? In what ways and situations have you heard it applied?

Normally, we apply this promise to maintaining the faith in spite of obstacles. We don't view it as pertaining to evangelism or missions. But look at the preceding words: "I always pray with joy because of your partnership in the gospel from the first day until now, being confident of this, that he who began a good work..." (Phil. 1:4-6). Paul the Missionary had planted the gospel in Philippi (Acts 16:11-40). Because the Philippians supported Paul's mission work, he calls them "partners in the gospel." Thus, the context of the promise in Phil. 1:6 is Christian outreach.

Also, we tend to apply Phil. 1:6 individually. Since God began a good work in you (singular) when He saved you (singular), He won't abandon you (singular). However, "you" in this verse is plural. While the promise may be applied individually, Paul originally spoke it to a congregation. Christian outreach works best as a team sport, not an individual one. The basic team is you and your church.

An example. I know a church which began almost seventy years ago. For decades they had abundant energy and vision. Their buildings bustled with activity. Today, the neighborhood is changing, the members are growing old, and discouragement is mounting. On the basis of Philippians 1:6, I counseled them: "The Lord has started a good work of salvation and outreach in every local church. It never needs to peter out. God promises He will fulfill His purpose for your church. So don't give up!"

What hope does the outreach promise in Philippians 1:6 offer to your church about its outreach strategy, team spirit, and future dreams? ✏️

So-called hopeless cases. In Matthew 19:26, Jesus promises, "With God all things are possible." Christians quote this optimistic phrase left and right. In what ways and situations have you heard this promise applied?

Normally, Christians generalize Matthew 19:26, applying it to almost everything. This is permissible, but consider the context in which Jesus spoke the promise. He had just told the rich young ruler, "Go, sell your possessions and give to the poor, and you will have treasure in heaven. Then come, follow me" (Mt. 19:21). When the fellow preferred to keep his riches, Jesus said, "It is easier for a camel to go through the eye of a needle than for a rich man to enter the kingdom of heaven" (Mt. 19:24). When His disciples asked, "Then who can be saved?", He promised, "With man this is impossible, but with God all things are possible" (Mt. 19:26).

This verse does not mean that everyone to whom you witness will be converted, but it does speak to when we mistakenly assume that someone's conversion is impossible. In Matthew 19:26,

Jesus promises the Holy Spirit can convert so-called hopeless cases, even the abrasive persons who berate you and your Savior.

Who are the unsaved people you are concerned about who consider themselves too rich, too intelligent, or too talented to surrender all and follow Christ? How does Jesus' outreach promise "with God all things are possible" strengthen you to reach out to them? ⬅

Prayer: Holy Spirit, You alone convert people's hearts. Help me to trust in Your power and Your compassion.

Action: Study your favorite promises in their biblical context. You may discover they are good stings for Christian outreach.

C. Overflowing with Living Water

A missionary to Japan told me about a profound conversation between two Japanese believers. The ideas exchanged between them are dramatized in the following fictional account.

Timely questions. Rieko and Suzuki-san had spent a pleasant morning hiking in the mountains. Now they relaxed at a small restaurant beside a mountain stream.

Once the food was served, Suzuki-san spoke up. "Rieko, my dear," she addressed the younger woman affectionately, "I invited you on this excursion, because recently you appear less cheerful in your faith. Am I correct about this? Is something wrong?"

"You know me well, Suzuki-san. Six months ago, I confessed faith in God and was baptized into His holy name. What joy I had then," Rieko's eyes danced, and she giggled as you might expect from a teenager, which she was. Then her eyes dimmed, "But in the last month, my life in Christ has seemed dry, predictable—"

"And stagnant?" the older woman ventured.

"Yes, that's the perfect word. How did you know?"

"I have seen it before in other new believers. Some have drifted far from their Savior. I don't want that to happen to you, Rieko. May I share some wisdom with you?"

"Yes, please do."

"Diligently you have worked to fill your heart with Bible verses, hymns, doctrines, and prayers. But now you say you feel stagnant." Suzuki-san lifted the teapot, "More tea?"

"Yes, please."

The older woman filled Rieko's cup. Then she proceeded to fill her own cup, pouring and pouring, until a considerable amount had overflowed onto the table cloth. Rieko looked away, embarrassed for the ineptitude of her elder.

"Which teacup are you?" Suzuki-san quizzed.

Flustered, Rieko asked, "What do you mean?"

"Rieko, you are like your cup here, filled to the brim with truths about the Lord. But Christ provides you with enough to overflow, as my cup has done. He said, 'Whoever believes in me, as the Scripture has said, streams of living water will flow from within him' (Jn. 7:38-39). This refers to the Holy Spirit. Christ also said, 'I have come that they may have life, and have it to the full' (Jn. 10:10). 'To the full' means to have a surplus, more than you need for yourself. Our Lord supplies you plentifully so that you are free to overflow, to splash the life you have been given on those you know. Living this way, the Holy Spirit will refresh both you and others, and your faith will not be stagnant."

Suzuki-san paused, giving Rieko time to reflect. For a few minutes the young woman gazed at the rushing stream by their side. "I think I understand," her face brightened. "If this stream were damned up, it would become polluted, but as long as it flows, it remains pure. God placed His Holy Spirit in me not for me to hoard, but to flow through me to others. But how do I do that, Suzuki-san? Speaking up about Jesus is hard for me."

"Often Christians think that sharing their faith requires always saying the perfect thing at the perfect time. That is too difficult for us. We never learn perfectly, and the perfect moment never seems to come. So we say nothing."

"I have made that mistake," Rieko admitted. "So what is the right way?"

"Witnessing is far more than a human activity. It is God's work done through us. Witnessing is yielding ourselves to Christ and to the Holy Spirit, so they may testify through us."

Supporting verses. Suzuki-san led Rieko through a discussion of several more verses, including these.

I will pour our my Spirit on all people. Your sons and daughters will prophesy, your old men will dream dreams, your young men will see visions. Even on my servants, both men and women, I will pour out my Spirit (Joel 2:28-29).

I am the vine; you are the branches. If a man remains in me and I in him, he will bear much fruit; apart from me you can do nothing (Jn. 15:5).

You will receive power when the Holy Spirit comes on you; and you will be my witnesses in Jerusalem... and to the ends of the earth (Acts 1:8).

Then the nations will know that I am the LORD, declares the Sovereign LORD, when I show myself holy through you before their eyes (Ezek. 36:23).

With each verse Suzuki-san stressed that, while Christians play an active role in testifying about Christ, God Himself is the main actor. She concluded, "Rieko, we are like someone following the lead of a dance partner. We don't need to *do* witnessing; we simply *are* His witnesses, as we follow His lead. Do you understand how this takes the pressure off of us?"

"Yes, I think so. But I have one other concern. I am only one person. We Christians in Japan are barely one percent of the population. So much needs to be done to reach so many. I feel like I should be doing the work of a hundred persons, but I don't know if I can bear such a burden."

"Then give it to God, who alone can bear it." Suzuki-san looked past the hills to a dark blue line on the distant horizon. "Isn't it amazing, Rieko," she reflected, how this little mountain stream fills the whole Pacific Ocean.

Rieko laughed, "You are playing games with me again. This little stream doesn't fill the ocean. On our hike we crossed a dozen streams. There are thousands of them in Japan and millions in other lands. It takes many streams to fill the ocean."

"You are but one stream from which God's Spirit flows. God does not call you to fill the ocean of need in Japan or in the whole world. He only calls you to refresh those you pass along your way. If we all do our one-stream-sized part, God will accomplish His plan to refresh the nations."

"Your wise words remind me of a verse I love: 'For the earth will be filled with the knowledge of the glory of the LORD, as the waters cover the sea' (Hab. 2:14)."

"How true," Suzuki-san agreed. "Thank you, Rieko, for splashing that promise on me."

Prayer: Lord, cause me to overflow with Your life and Your love.

Action: Whenever you face a witnessing opportunity, remind yourself, "This is a job for God—who works through me."

D. A New Spirit for All Ages

What is the optimum age for doing evangelism? Some young people say, "Let older people do it. They have more experience." Some older people say, "Let younger people do it. They have more energy." But what does God promise you?

Youth. When God called Jeremiah to be a prophet, he objected to the assignment, "Ah, Sovereign LORD, I do not know how to speak; I am only a child" (Jer. 1:6). But the Lord assured him, "Do not be afraid of them, for I am with you and will rescue you.... Today I have made you a fortified city, an iron pillar and a bronze wall to stand against the whole land" (Jer. 1:8, 18).

God addressed Jeremiah's sense of outreach inadequacy through this promise. It also speaks to young Christians who feel as Jeremiah did.

Maturity. The viewpoint of an older believer is expressed in Psalm 71. Circle the words below which describe three different stages of life: youth, the present moment, and future old age.

Since my youth, O God, you have taught me, and to this day I declare your marvelous deeds. Even when I am old and gray, do not forsake me, O God, till I declare your power to the next generation, your might to all who are to come (Ps. 71:17-18).

The psalmist never intends to retire from being God's witness. His attitude is an encouragement to all older Christians.

Questions. How can the young be adequate witnesses in spite of their immaturity? How can adults be adequate witnesses in spite of their diminishing strength?

The answer appears in words which Paul, an older witness, addressed to Timothy, a younger witness. Paul wrote, "For God did not give us a spirit of timidity, but a spirit of power, of love and of self-discipline. So do not be ashamed to testify about our Lord, or ashamed of me his prisoner" (2 Tim. 1:7-8).

Paul writes from prison. He will soon be martyred for his faith in Christ. Timothy will have to persevere as persecution blazes. If Paul's promise is true in such perilous straits, surely it applies in our evangelism and mission endeavors as well.

A spirit of timidity does not come from God. It is part of our sinful nature which doubts God. Has a spirit of timidity ever made itself evident as you faced opportunities to spread the good news? What sort of witnessing occurs when timidity reigns?

A new spirit. To counter our timidity, Paul says God has given us a new spirit capable of rising above shame, eager to testify about our Lord. This spirit has three attributes.

1. A spirit of power. The Greek word is *dynamus* from which we get dynamite and dynamo. In Romans 1:16, Paul calls the gospel "the power [*dynamus*] of God." This is the kind of spirit the Holy Spirit has placed within you.

2. A spirit of love. The Greek word is *agape* which means unconditional love. In John 3:16, it says, "God so loved [*agaped*] the world that he gave his only Son." This is the kind of spirit the Holy Spirit has placed within you.

3. A spirit of self-discipline. The rare Greek word *sophronismos* means the ability to keep a cool head amid tense circumstances. This is the kind of spirit the Holy Spirit has placed within you.

Positive self-talk. Remember our friend Gertrude from Germany? When she failed to witness to her boss, Herr Lochner, she scolded herself, "You coward! You're hopeless!" Many Christians habitually berate themselves this way. No wonder they lack self-confidence to speak the name of Christ to others.

What would happen if you replaced such negative self-talk with positive truths from outreach promises? Every day tell yourself this: "I am a new creation in Christ; the old is gone, the new has come!" (2 Cor. 5:17). Whenever you have an opportunity to share Christ, remind yourself: "God did not give me a spirit of timidity, but a spirit of power, of love and of self-discipline. So I am not ashamed to testify about my Lord" (2 Tim. 1:7-8).

What outreach ventures are you willing to attempt, knowing God has given you a spirit of power, love, and self-discipline?

Prayer: Lord, thanks for equipping me at every stage of my life.
Action: Begin to practice positive self-talk as described above.

E. Best Case Scenarios

He vowed he was willing to die for Christ.
Then he was alone fearing enemies on every side.
He was offered a chance to declare his faith in Christ.
But he denied he had ever met his Lord.
When the rooster crowed, he wept bitterly.

This story is no outreach promise. It's an outreach disaster! It makes us quiver and question: "If Peter, Jesus' most solid disciple, cracked under pressure, what hope is there for me?"

Worst-case scenarios. Why did Peter falter? When he imagined what would happen, all he could picture was rejection and danger. He was incapacitated by his worst-case scenarios.

Use your imagination for a moment. What bad things might have occurred if Peter had spoken up about Christ?

Think of a time when you lacked the courage to witness. What worst-case scenarios hampered you?

Best-case scenarios. Use your imagination again, but this time focus on best-case scenarios. What good things might have occurred if Peter had witnessed about Christ?

Worst-case scenarios paralyze us. Best-case scenarios motivate us to take risks. God's outreach promises are best-case scenarios. Read the following promises and apply them to an outreach frustration you presently are facing. Perhaps they will help you picture a best-case scenario.

The [gospel] promise is for you and your children and for all who are far off—for all whom the Lord our God will call (Acts 2:39).

Salvation is found in no one else, for there is no other name under heaven by which we must be saved (Acts 4:12. Hint: invert the thought to a positive statement.).

But you are a chosen people, a royal priesthood, a holy nation, a people belonging to God, that you might declare the praises of him who called you out of darkness into his marvelous light (1 Pt. 2:9).

Live such good lives among the pagans that, though they accuse you of doing wrong, they may see your good deeds and glorify God on the day he visits us (1 Pt. 2:12).

Wives, in the same way be submissive to your husbands so that, if any of them do not believe the word, they may be won over without words by the behavior of their wives, when they see the purity and reverence of your lives (1 Pt. 3:1-2).

What best-case scenario occurred to you as you reflected on these verses?

A surprise. Did you notice who stated all these outreach promises? Peter. The same fellow who denied Christ later proclaimed Him boldly and taught others to do the same.

Wow! Peter rose from tragedy to triumph, because Christ, in His grace and mercy, restored Peter as His disciple. Perhaps even Peter's outreach disaster is a sort of round-about outreach promise. If Christ could restore him, then He will restore you too when you repent of your failures to share His love.

Prayer: Father, remove my blindness to the good results You intend to accomplish through my simple witness.

Action: Begin to act upon the best-case scenario you visualized.

5 OUTREACH PROMISES AND MISSION WORK

As you share Christ with people nearby, God will broaden your horizons to see His love for all people in every place. Although cross-cultural evangelistic work is daunting, God's outreach promises assure you it can be done and will be done.

A. Expanding Your Family Photo Album

Picture this. Imagine a family photo album containing pictures of the entire Christian Church. Look, there are the folks in your home church. And over here are the faces of brothers and sisters from all over the world—every man, woman, and child who confesses Christ. And still the family photo album is incomplete. Many empty pages remain, awaiting photos of countless not-yet brothers and not-yet sisters who still need to hear the gospel.

Infertility. Our global family began with Abraham and Sarah, a barren couple to whom the Lord promised, "I will make you into a great nation .... and all people on earth will be blessed through you" (Gen. 12:2,3). "Look up at the heavens and count the stars .... So shall your offspring be" (Gen. 15:5). But for years after receiving these promises, Abraham and Sarah remained childless. Surely, they mourned their barrenness.

Infertile couples who wish to have children mourn the death of their dream of raising a family. As you look at your participation in witnessing and global missions, do you ever feel sort of barren and childless? Do you accept this barrenness as normal, or do you consider it contrary to God's will? ⮕

Thicker than water. In spite of their infertility, finally God gave Abraham and Sarah the child He had promised. They named him Isaac, which means "laughter." Joy abounds when a child is born, especially after a long wait, and no one waited longer than Abraham and Sarah.

God compares evangelism to the growth of a global family. We see this in three texts from Isaiah which foretell Israel's redemption from exile in Babylon and restoration as a nation. However, the global details in these prophecies seem to point beyond the restoration of Israel to God's plan to raise up children of Abraham from among all nations (Gal. 3:6-9, 26-29).

Listen to the Lord's joy at expanding the family photo album. He sounds like a parent shouting, "It's a girl!" or "It's a boy!"

> I will bring your children from the east and gather them from the west. I will say to the north, "Give them up!" and to the south, "Do not hold them back." Bring my sons from afar and my daughters from the ends of the earth—everyone who is called by my name, whom I created for my glory... (Is. 43:5-7).

> Then you will say in your heart, "Who bore me these? I was bereaved and barren; I was exiled and rejected.... but these—where have they come from?" This is what the Sovereign Lord says: "See, I will beckon to the Gentiles, I will lift up my banner [meaning Christ] to the peoples; they will bring your sons in their arms and carry your daughters on their shoulders" (Is. 49:21-22).

> Lift up your eyes and look about you... your sons come from afar, and your daughters are carried on the arm. Then you will look and be radiant, your heart will throb and swell with joy (Is. 60:4-5).

In English we say "blood is thicker than water," which means family is the highest allegiance. In these promises God arouses your profound, innate dedication to family, so that you will do all you can to add your not-yet sisters and not-yet brothers to the family photo album of those justified by faith in Jesus Christ.

Prayer: Thank You for placing me in Your global, growing family.

Action: Collect pictures of people from many lands. Place them in an album or collage. Let the pictures remind you of your family.

B. Harmony in the Multicultural Church

Culture shock. Are you uncomfortable with other cultures? Most folks are. Picture the ministry of Carl and Karol Selle, missionaries to international students on campuses in the USA. They meet students from Japan, China, India, Zaire, Pakistan, Egypt, Brazil, Colombia, Russia, Romania, and so on. Imagine the mind-boggling variety of ethnic foods, music, arts, folklore, governments, social customs, values, and religious traditions. When converts from these many cultures try to worship and serve God together, disagreements may arise and divide them into separate ethnic enclaves.

Our fearful response to multi-cultural outreach may be, "Why can't everyone else speak my language, eat my food, and sing my hymns? Why can't everyone be my culture?"

Have you ever felt this way? Would you feel better if you knew the existence of many cultures was actually part of God's plan? It is! Revelation 21:26 says, "The glory and honor of the nations will be brought into it [the new Jerusalem]."

Plenty of time. What are the glory and honor of a nation? A nation's language, music, art, science, and knowledge. We lump these glories together in one word—culture!

God not only declares individuals to be holy saints, in Revelation 21:26 He promises to sanctify our cultures as well. Although all human cultures (including your own) are tainted with much that is impure, shameful, and deceitful, none of this will be allowed entrance into heaven. However, everything which is glorious and honorable in each nation will be brought into the new Jerusalem as tribute to its King, the Triune Savior God.

In the 1960s, Black singer Aretha Franklin released her first hits. Her Afro-American music sounded foreign to my Euro-American ears. But when Aretha's fifth song hit the charts, I heard it on the radio one day and said to myself, "You know, *this*

Aretha Franklin song isn't bad at all. She must be getting better."
Then I listened a little closer and realized it was *not* her latest
release. The song I was praising was her first record which I had
hated two years earlier. Who had changed: Aretha or me?

Recently my wife and I attended a gathering of Asian Indians.
After hours of music and dancing which seemed strange to us,
we admitted, "It would take a long time to get used to this culture."

Well, in heaven how much time will we have to learn to appreciate the thousands of cultures which will be represented there?
We will have all eternity. Heaven will hum with multicultural harmony. Right now you may not like Indian music or Japanese the-
ater or Bolivian dance, which are the cultural glories of those
people. But in heaven what you now call "foreign" you will learn
to love, as you experience it being used to glorify the Savior of
the nations. Meanwhile, your music and art will be prized by the
citizens of heaven from other cultures.

What culture or different environment do you need to grow to
appreciate? How does God's promise of multi-cultural harmony
in heaven liberate you to steadily learn and become comfortable
with that culture this side of heaven? ✏️

Shoulder to shoulder. Here is a wonderful promise about
multicultural ministry. "Then I will purify the lips of the peoples,
that all of them may call on the name of the LORD and serve him
shoulder to shoulder. From beyond the rivers of Cush [the upper
Nile region] my worshipers, my scattered people, will bring me
offerings" (Zeph. 3:9-10).

The phrase "shoulder to shoulder" is a powerful image imply-
ing intimate proximity, concerted strength, and unified purpose.
To serve God in this way with folks from other cultures is a joy-
ous experience, but sometimes we miss out on it.

Once I painted some rooms at an inner-city church used by
two congregations, one English-speaking the other Spanish-
speaking. As I painted, I listened to the church members talking
about their brothers and sisters in the other language group.
They were experiencing severe cultural tensions over the main-
tenance of the building. How Satan must snicker when petty disagreements divide the unity God has given us in Christ.

Perhaps you know of a multi-cultural outreach effort which is floundering because the people involved fail to understand each other's cultures. This occurs far too often. In stark contrast, when believers from different ethnic groups learn to serve God "shoulder to shoulder," they delight in God-given solidarity.

Have you ever known the joy of serving God with people from other cultures? Have you ever longed for such unity of heart and purpose? In Zeph. 3:9-10, the Lord promises this blessing to His international church. On the basis of this promise, what steps toward shared ministry are you willing to take? ⊜>

Prayer: Thank You for cultures, Lord. Help me enjoy the variety.

Action: With a Christian from a different culture than yours, discuss how you both can better serve God shoulder to shoulder.

C. Promises for Challenging Fields

Christian outreach is not only cross-cultural. It is also cross-environmental. As you share Christ, the Holy Spirit may give you adventures in challenging new settings. But fear not! God has given outreach promises for these environments too.

Urban. Mission work is not limited to jungles, deserts, and rural areas. Of the over two billion people who have never heard the gospel, over half live in cities. Cities everywhere are growing. This troubles rural and suburban Christians who tend to view the city as an evil, distasteful environment for evangelism efforts. What are your experiences and opinions about urban outreach?

Here is a promise God gave about urban ministry: "Many peoples and the inhabitants of many cities will yet come, and the inhabitants of one city will go to another and say, 'Let us go at once to entreat the LORD and seek the LORD Almighty. I myself am going'" (Zech. 8:20-21).

This prophecy was fulfilled in the centuries immediately before Christ's coming. During that era, Jews spread throughout the ancient world and drew many Gentiles to their synagogues. Today, God is urbanizing the world as never before. If we enter our cities to serve in Christ's name, surely the Lord can accomplish again what He promised.

May Zechariah 8:20-21 and promises like it speak to your fears and misgivings about urban outreach.

The powerless. Suppose you had a chance to reach out in Christ's name to people who were poor, crippled, blind, or lame. You might hesitate at the difficulty of entering their unique environments. But consider Jesus' parable of the great banquet. After the privileged guests refused to attend, the owner of the house ordered his servant, "Go out quickly into the streets and alleys of the town and bring in the poor, the crippled, the blind and the lame" (Lk. 14:21). The servant obeyed, and the new invitees gladly came to the banquet.

What does this parable promise Christians who venture into the environment of powerless and needy people? To what personal witnessing opportunity might you apply this promise?

The powerful. Most Christians feel outmatched sharing their faith with powerful people. This was the assignment given to Daniel and his friends Shadrach, Meshach, and Abednego in the royal courts of Babylon. After many struggles the Lord turned the heart of proud King Nebuchadnezzar. Daniel 4 contains the marvelous testimony of faith which Nebuchadnezzar sent "to the peoples, nations and men of every language who live in all the world" (Dan. 4:1). This story is a promise of hope for all believers seeking to reach the powerful and influential of the world.

The sexually damaged. Sex is a gift from God, but humans have so twisted it that many people are sexually crippled. This difficult environment includes the sexually abused, pornography addicts, pimps and prostitutes, practicing homosexuals and lesbians, and others. Can such people be reached with the gospel? Yes, for God promised,

> To the eunuchs [castrated men] who keep my sabbaths, who choose what pleases me and hold fast to my covenant—to them I will give within my temple and its walls a memorial and a name better than sons and daughters; I will give them an everlasting name that will not be cut off (Is. 56:4-5).

What a marvelous promise for eunuchs and, by logical extension, for all sexually damaged people. Note the play on words in "a name better" than children that will "not be cut off." In Acts 8:26-40 this promise was fulfilled by the conversion of the Ethiopian eunuch, and it still continues to be fulfilled today.

Use the promise in Isaiah 56:4-5 to encourage you to share Christ's love with sexually damaged people.

Prayer: Wherever I serve in Your name, Your promises precede me.

Action: Identify the environments you enter for the sake of the gospel. As you read the Bible, look for promises for each setting.

D. Temples on the Go

Here is how some churches do evangelism: "We hold worship services every Sunday. If people want to come, they are welcome." Outreach promises using temple imagery offer us a much more proactive and mobile strategy than this.

The role of a temple. At the dedication of the first Jewish temple, King Solomon prayed that foreigners would come from distant lands to the temple to pray. "Do whatever the foreigner asks of you, so that all the peoples of the earth may know your name and fear you" (1 Kings 8:43). This petition shows that the evangelistic purpose of a temple is to draw unreached people to God. However, Solomon subverted this strategy by building temples to other gods for his foreign wives (1 Kings 11:1-10). When the idolatry increased, God let enemies destroy Solomon's temple.

Despite this disaster, God promised He would use a temple to draw distant people to himself. For example Isaiah 56:6-7 says,

> And foreigners who bind themselves to the LORD to serve him, to love the name of the LORD, and to worship him,.... these I will bring to my holy mountain and give them joy in my house of prayer.... for my house will be called a house of prayer for all nations (See also Ezek. 37:24-28.).

Human temples. Later on, Christ fulfilled the symbolism of the temple sacrificial system. With His one perfect sacrifice for sins, and with the destruction of Herod's temple by the Romans in A.D. 70, we might assume God had abandoned the use of temples. However, Paul the Missionary taught otherwise. God is still in the temple business, although His strategy is new.

> Don't you know that you yourselves are God's temple and that God's Spirit lives in you? (1 Cor. 3:16).

> For we are the temple of the living God. As God has said: "I will live with them and walk among them, and I will be their God, and they will be my people" (2 Cor. 6:16; see Ezek. 37:27).

A temple is a place where God dwells. Peter taught that the Holy Spirit dwells in us through baptism (Acts 2:38). This is awesome! People everywhere are looking for God, and He dwells inside of you and me.

Temples on the move. God's plan for the nations revolves around the words "apostle" and "missionary" which mean "one who is sent." In the Old Testament God promised He would use temples to reach the nations. But temples of wood and stone can't be sent anywhere, because they're fixed to the ground.

However, temples of flesh and blood and Holy Spirit are a different story. You and I, who are God's temples, *can* be sent. You are God's portable temple, a new and improved model compared to the temples of former eras.

As God's temple, what can you do that the old stone temples could never accomplish? Out of all the possible places God might send you, His portable temple, where and to whom might He lead you today? Next month? Next year? ▷

Court of the Gentiles. When Jesus cleansed the temple, He quoted the outreach promise we read earlier in Isaiah 56:7, saying, "Is it not written: 'My house will be called a house of prayer for all nations'? But you have made it 'a den of robbers.'" (Mk. 11:17). The part of the temple the merchants had seized was called the court of the Gentiles, a spacious area reserved for welcoming visitors from outside Judaism. Jesus cleared this area, so foreigner visitors to the temple would be welcomed properly.

Figuratively speaking, what is your personal court of the Gentiles, the way you welcome outsiders? What is your church's court of the Gentiles? Think beyond the architecture of your building to the attitudes and activities of your church members. What obstacles and distractions might the Lord need to clear out? ▣⇒

Prayer: O God, may Your Spirit in me show through to others.

Action: God intends you to be a mobile temple. Identify ways you tend to be too rooted. Where might He want you to venture?

E. Mission Promised, Mission Possible

Mission Impossible? Nearly two thousand years ago, Christ told us to make disciples of all nations. Today, each person who confesses Christ is proof of the progress of the gospel.

But so much remains to be done. To many people God's mission seems impossible. Place a ✔ beside the obstacles below which increase your outreach doubts, fears, and discouragement.

__ Your own limited ability to love others and witness to them
__ Fellow Christians who seem unconcerned about the lost
__ So many sinful lifestyles
__ So many excuses for ignoring Christ and the gospel
__ So many disagreements and divisions between Christians
__ So many people in the world—nearly six billion
__ So many languages—over seven thousand
__ So many strange cultures
__ So many false gods and religions
__ So many hostile governments
__ Satan and his deceiving demons

Mission Promised. In spite of these obstacles, some Christians are crazy enough to continue with God's mission. They identify the remaining unreached people groups. They develop strategies to send missionaries to each people group. They recruit and send missionaries. They learn the language and culture. They pray for conversions. They teach the converts to share their new faith with others, until everyone in that people group may hear the good news God prepared for them two thousand years ago.

What motivates this crazy mission behavior? Don't they know the mission is impossible? No! They know exactly the opposite. God promised His global task could be done. So they conclude: Mission promised, mission possible.

You don't have to be insane to participate in world evangelization. You only have to be confident that what God has promised He will accomplish.

Promise upon promise. Sometimes, in order for us to grasp a biblical truth, we need to hear it echo repeatedly. May each of the ten verses below be like the hammer blow of a diamond cutter, so that every facet of God's mission glitters with certainty.

1. Look up at the heavens and count the stars—if indeed you can count them. So shall your offspring be (Gen. 15:5; God speaking to Abram).

2. The LORD your God has increased your numbers so that today you are as many as the stars in the sky. May the Lord, the God of your fathers, increase you a thousand times and bless you as he has promised! (Dt. 1:10-11).

3. He put a new song in my mouth, a hymn of praise to our God. Many will see and fear and put their trust in the LORD (Ps. 40:3).

4. The nobles of the nations assemble as the people of the God of Abraham, for the kings of the earth belong to God; he is greatly exalted (Ps. 47:9).

5. May all the kings of the earth praise you, O LORD, when they hear the words of your mouth (Ps. 138:4).

6. The fruit of the righteous is a tree of life; and he who wins souls is wise.... There is no wisdom, no insight, no plan that can succeed against the LORD (Prov. 11:30; 21:30).

7. It is too small a thing for you [Christ] to be my servant to restore the tribes of Jacob and bring back those of Israel I have kept. I will also make you a light for the

Gentiles, that you may bring my salvation to the ends of the earth (Is. 49:6).

8. As the rain and the snow come down from heaven, and do not return to it without watering the earth and making it bud and flourish, so that it yields seed for the sower and bread for the eater, so is my word that goes out from my mouth: It will not return to me empty, but will accomplish what I desire and achieve the purpose for which I sent it (Is. 55:10-11).

9. O LORD,... to you the nations will come from the ends of the earth and say, "Our fathers possessed nothing but false gods, worthless idols that did them no good. Do men make their own gods? Yes, but they are not gods!" "Therefore I will teach them—this time I will teach them my power and might. Then they will know that my name is the LORD" (Jer. 16:19-21).

10. See, your king comes to you, righteous and having salvation, gentle and riding on a donkey,... He will proclaim peace to the nations. His rule will extend from sea to sea and from the River to the ends of the earth (Zech. 9:9-10).

These selections are from the Old Testament only. The New Testament is similarly rich in outreach promises. If God had stated only once or twice that He intended to extend His kingdom to all nations, would you conclude He was serious about it? Maybe not.

But what if the Lord said it again and again, and phrased it in a variety of emphatic ways? A missionary friend once told me, "Ever since you introduced me to outreach promises, I keep finding more and more. In my quiet time, I'm constantly shouting, 'There's another one!'"

The sheer volume of outreach promises speaks volumes about God's dedication to reach all nations. The message is clear: Mission promised, mission possible.

Prayer: Lord, may your mission promises give me confidence to serve in Christ's name wherever Your Spirit leads me.

Action: Select a promise in this section and learn it by heart.

And when the strife is fierce, the warfare long,
Steals on the ear the distant triumph song,
and hearts are brave again and arms are strong.
Alleluia! Alleluia!

6 *FACING OBSTACLES AND OPPONENTS*

Do outreach promises transform witnessing and missions into safe endeavors involving little risk or danger? Not at all. However, our truthful God never soft pedals the difficulty of His rescue work, nor does He abandon you when you grow weary.

A. Realistic Recruitment

Unrealistic recruitment. Have you ever received a phone call like this? "Hi, this is Joe from church. I'm recruiting volunteers to help with activity X. Could you help us?"

You ask, "How much time and effort will activity X take?"

"Oh, not much. It'll be easy."

Now, which is most likely to occur?:

___ a. Activity X will be less work than was claimed.
___ b. Activity X will be as much work as was claimed.
___ c. Activity X will be more work than was claimed.

Let's face it. Some tasks become more than we bargained for.

Honest recruitment. Our Lord is seeking people like you to share His love and proclaim the gospel near and far. Unlike a volunteer hunter who soft-pedals the difficulty of a task, our God is totally honest about the hazards and the opposition.

For example, in 2 Corinthians 6:4-5 Paul lists nine difficulties he faces: troubles, hardships, distresses, beatings, imprisonments, riots, hard work, sleepless nights, and hunger. Is this a gripe list? No, it is the job description of a Christian witness. Paul's honesty shows God is a realist, not some lunatic dreamer. Even texts like 2 Corinthians 6:4-5, which describe the difficulty of sharing the faith, are outreach promises, because in them God promises we will be opposed by the world, our flesh, and the devil.

Similar problems confront missionaries today. Nurse Gloria Sauck serves the Samburu people of Kenya. Like Paul, she has endured nine difficulties: robbery, car jacking, threat of rape, hepatitis, malaria, a bus accident, the near loss of her leg, and being dragged across rocks by a run-away camel. To top it all off, her only missionary co-worker was unexpectedly called home to heaven. These are enough tribulations for a lifetime, but Gloria experienced them all during her first four-year term in Kenya.

Promises for every difficulty. How does God ever get anyone to volunteer for His mission? Well, in addition to being honest about the difficulty, the Lord graciously counters every outreach challenge with a corresponding outreach promise. Consider this list from 2 Corinthians. Underline the items which are most pertinent to your witnessing circumstances.

We are hard pressed on every side, but not crushed;
> perplexed, but not in despair;
> persecuted, but not abandoned;
> struck down, but not destroyed" (4:8-9).
[We are] genuine, yet regarded as impostors;
> known, yet regarded as unknown;
> dying, and yet we live on;
> beaten, and yet not killed;
> sorrowful, yet always rejoicing;
> poor, yet making many rich;
> having nothing, and yet possessing everything (6:8-10).

What powerful contrasts! No matter what hardships may arise, God counteracts and overcomes them with His mercies. May Paul's pithy promises of hope speak to your troubled heart.

More promises. Texts like Matthew 10 and 24, Luke 10, and all the Book of Revelation overflow with outreach promises to strenghten us in the face of fierce opposition from Satan and unbelievers. For example, Jesus said, "But when they arrest you, do not worry about what to say or how to say it. At that time you will be given what to say" (Mt. 10:19). Our Lord is a realistic recruiter who honestly admits the work is hard but compassionately matches every potential obstacle with a promise.

Prayer: When I feel forsaken, remind me I am held in Your hands.

Action: Identify a time you volunteered for a difficult church task. How might outreach promises have helped you?

B. Taking the Offensive

Satan, the Discourager. God isn't the only one sending out missionaries. 2 John 7 says, "Many deceivers, who do not acknowledge Jesus Christ as coming in the flesh, have gone out into the world. Any such person is the deceiver and the antichrist." Satan is always recruiting false teachers to "blind the eyes of unbelievers" (2 Cor.4:4) with his deceptions and lies.

How can we stand against such an opponent? In Matthew 16:16, Peter confesses Jesus is "the Christ, the Son of the living God." Then the Lord responds,

> I tell you that you are Peter, and on this rock I will build my church, and the gates of Hades will not overcome it [or the gates of Hades will not prove stronger than it]. I will give you the keys of the kingdom of heaven; whatever you bind on earth will be bound in heaven, and whatever you loose on earth will be loosed in heaven (16:18-19).

These verses contain three outreach promises to help us stand against Satan and all opponents.

Master Builder. Building a global church of believers from every tribe, language, people, and nation is a tall order. But ultimately, this construction project is not our doing. According to the words: "On this rock I will build my church," the one who builds the worldwide church is Christ, not we His witnesses.

What is the church's foundation? Roman Catholicism believes "this rock" refers to Peter and the future papacy. Protestantism believes "this rock" is the solid truth Peter confessed: "You are the Christ." This confession is the foundation of the Christian faith.

Christ, the Master Builder, builds His church on Himself. This is a relief to all of us whom He involves in the project.

Stronger than Hades. The gates of Hades refers to Satan and all the demons at his beck and call. These thugs constantly oppose the building of Christ's church. In Matthew 16:18 Jesus promises victory over them in words which can be translated in two equally valid ways. Both translations teach a useful lesson.

"The gates of Hades will not overcome it [the church]" is defensive. When Satan attacks the church, we will not fall.

What consolation do you draw from the defensive version of this promise? ▱▷

"The gates of Hades will not prove stronger than it [the church]." This statement is offensive. When Christians attack and storm the kingdom of Satan, the church will overpower it.

What confidence do you gain from the offensive version of this promise? ▱▷

Weapons. To attack the gates of Hades, we had better have good weapons. Jesus arms us for battle in the very next sentence, "I will give you the keys of the kingdom of heaven" (v. 19).

What? We fight the evil forces of Hades with keys? That's right! But no keys are like these keys.

One key locks and binds. It is the message of God's judgment on rebellion, sin, and injustice. When we announce this to proud and unrepentant people, it shows them the door of heaven is locked to them. This key is the Law of God.

The other key unlocks and frees. It is the message of Christ's redeeming sacrifice and resurrection. When we announce this to the humbled and repentant, they can rejoice that their sins are forgiven and the doors of heaven are open to them. This key is the Gospel.

Equipped with these keys, what territory of Satan can you invade for Christ?

Prayer: Lord, thanks for Your weapons, the keys of the Kingdom.

Action: Pray for God to unlock the heart of someone presently closed to His truth.

C. Getting Across the Lake

A riddle. Most people know the answer to the question: Why did the chicken cross the road? It's a lame, old joke. But in the familiar story of Jesus stilling the storm, why did Jesus and His disciples cross the lake?

Most of us think the story ends with them sailing on placid waters. But let's learn the complete story from Mark 4:35-5:20. Jesus was leading His disciples on a mission adventure. Three times they are attacked, but each time He leads them to victory.

The mission field. Some people mistakenly assume a missionary's major role is to bring advanced culture and technology to underprivileged people. If this were so, Jesus would have stayed on His side of the lake. The region across the Lake of Galilee was called the Decapolis, a Greek word meaning "Ten Towns." The people there were non-Jews. They were heirs of Greek culture, complete with all its great art, wisdom, philosophy, and religion. In spite of their advanced culture, the people in the Decapolis still lacked a saving relationship with God through faith in Jesus Christ.

What individuals or groups of people do you know who are well-cultured, but still lack such a relationship with God?

Attack #1. Have you ever wondered what caused the sudden, violent storm on the Lake of Galilee? Perhaps it was purely meteorological, but Job 1:18-19 records that Satan can produce fatal storms. Even though we can not prove it, the storm could have been Satan's attempt to send the boatload of missionaries to Davy Jones's locker, but Christ proved stronger.

What "storms" have risen to hinder your witnessing? What difference does it make to know that, like the disciples, you can call on Christ to still such "storms"? ✏️

Attack #2. After almost drowning, the disciples are starting to calm down now. They long for terra firma, but when they land, they find themselves in a graveyard in the middle of the night. Among the tombs is a naked, raving maniac who can tear them limb from limb. This isn't terra firma. It's terror! We aren't told what the disciples said, but we wouldn't hold it against them if they had screamed, "Jesus, let's get out of here!"

However, neither the disciples nor we understand Jesus' plan. The dangerous demoniac is the very individual Jesus came across the lake to meet. In this divine appointment, the Lord frees him from the Legion of demons that rule him. He is saved and restored.

Have you ever been in a witnessing situation that seemed as dangerous as this? If so, did you run, or did you stick around? Who are your difficult cases, people whom you consider too untamed to ever approach? Does Jesus consider them hopeless? Should you? ✏️

Attack #3. Things are looking up now. The maniac is clothed, in his right mind, and listening to Jesus. Maybe mission work isn't so bad after all. But then the neighbors show up. Fearing Jesus' power they order Him to leave. Jesus agrees to go.

"What?!" we protest. "After all this risk and bother, all we will have to show for it is one convert?"

But we are wrong. Jesus orders the man to go tell his family how the Lord has had mercy on him. The fellow obeys, proclaiming God's mercy throughout the Decapolis. When Jesus returns months later, the crowds welcome Him (Mk. 6:53-56).

What looked like a feeble skirmish into Satan's territory becomes a mighty blow.

Have you ever made small beginnings in witnessing to someone and then given up? Dream a moment. On the basis of this story, how might the tale of your initial efforts end? ✏️⟹

Prayer: Jesus, accompany me wherever I go to share Your name.

Action: Identify a "lake" which you could cross with Jesus' help.

D. Prayer Catalysts

One of the few facts you may recall from studying chemistry is that a catalyst is a substance which initiates a chemical reaction. Outreach promises are prayer catalysts to propel you into action.

Boldness. In Acts 4:23-31, when the early church faced rising persecution, they gathered to pray. Under similar circumstances, which petition below would you have prayed?

___ a. Lord, make our persecutors change their minds.

___ b. Strike our opponents with a plague.

___ c. Forgive us for not proclaiming Christ due to our fear.

___ d. Make us bold to speak your saving message.

Rejecting the cowardly options, they pleaded, "Lord,... enable your servants to speak your word with great boldness" (Acts 4:29). And it worked! "They were all filled with the Holy Spirit and spoke the word of God boldly" (Acts 4:31).

What had motivated them to pray for boldness? While they prayed they had quoted Psalm 2, which is both a messianic prophecy and an outreach prophecy. The psalm describes the triumph of God's global purposes despite the opposition of the world's kings and rulers. Encouraged by the optimism of Psalm 2, the believers asked for boldness. And they received it pronto!

So let outreach promises catalyze your prayers and those of your church. Here are some more outreach prayer catalysts.

Spiritual blindness. Are you disturbed about Satan's sway over people in Mongolia or Mexico or your own neighborhood?

Then pray on the basis of what Christ promised Paul in Acts 26:18. The Lord vowed "to open their eyes and turn them from darkness to light, and from the power of Satan to God...".

Using this promise as a catalyst, what does the Holy Spirit lead you to pray? ☞

Slip sliding away. If you are disappointed by Christians who stray from the faith, base your prayers on this promise: "I chose you and appointed you to go and bear fruit—*fruit that will last.* Then the Father will give you whatever you ask in my name" (Jn. 15:16; italics mine).

Using this promise as a catalyst, what does the Holy Spirit lead you to pray? ☞

Power shortage. Do you sense the need for the Holy Spirit to rejuvenate Christians with faith and fervency to share Christ? Then you are exactly like Moses who said, "I wish that all the LORD's people were prophets and that the LORD would put his Spirit on them!" (Num. 11:29). To all who share this desire, Jesus promised, "If you then, though you are evil, know how to give good gifts to your children, how much more will your Father in heaven give the Holy Spirit to those who ask him!" (Lk. 11:13).

Using this promise as a catalyst, what does the Holy Spirit lead you to pray? ☞

Doubts about prayer. Do you find it hard to pray about serving and reaching pre-Christians, because you wonder if God will respond? Meditate on John 14:13: "I [Christ] will do whatever you ask in my name, so that the Son may bring glory to the Father."

Using this promise as a catalyst, what does the Holy Spirit lead you to pray? ☞

The Second Lord's Prayer. What other outreach needs do you and your church have? Ask the Lord to lead you to corresponding outreach promises which will be catalysts for your bold petitions. A good place for finding such promises is The Second Lord's Prayer. I'm not joking. The Second Lord's Prayer is right there in John 17.

Jesus spoke this prayer on Maundy Thursday, shortly before He fulfilled the messianic prophecies about His death and rising. Knowing He soon would send His followers to all the world to fulfill God's outreach prophecies, the Lord stocked this prayer with plenty of outreach promises. Here are a few.

> I have given them your word and the world has hated them, for they are not of the world any more than I am of the world. My prayer is not that you take them out of the world but that you protect them from the evil one. They are not of the world, even as I am not of it. (Jn. 17:14-16)

> My prayer is not for them alone. I pray also for those who will believe in me through their message, that all of them may be one, Father, just as you are in me and I am in you. May they also be in us so that the world may believe that you have sent me. I have given them the glory that you gave me, that they may be one as we are one: I in them and you in me. May they be brought to complete unity to let the world know that you sent me and have loved them even as you have loved me (Jn. 17:20-23).

Prayer: Thank You, Jesus that You still pray in this manner today as You intercede for us at the right hand of God (Rom. 8:34).

Action: Select your favorite promises from the Second Lord's Prayer. Pray them often, as you do the First Lord's Prayer.

E. The Ruler of Every Moment

If you had an opportunity to change history, would you take it? Well, whenever you participate in sharing your faith and expanding God's kingdom, that is an opportunity to change history for individuals who do not yet know the Lord as Savior. Will you rise to the occasion, or will fear of unbelievers and the opposition of Satan cause you to miss your opportunities? To help answer this question, let's investigate Revelation 4 and 5.

In Revelation 4 God the Father reigns on His throne in glory and receives the worship of angels and twenty-four elders. I used to think the twenty-four elders represented deceased Christians already in heaven. I was wrong. The twenty-four elders represent the believers here on the earth during all ages of history. That means they also represent you and me and all believers alive at this very moment. Therefore, what the twenty-four elders do and say in Revelation 4 and 5 are *our* actions and *our* words.

Wow! Isn't it amazing to be innocently reading the Bible and suddenly realize you are one of the characters in the story?

Christ's role in history. Revelation 5:1-2 directs our attention to an unusual scroll.

> Then I saw in the right hand of him who sat on the throne a scroll with writing on both sides and sealed with seven seals. And I saw a mighty angel proclaiming, "Who is worthy to... open the scroll?"

The scroll represents the future events of history. Whoever receives it has authority to rule over all events, peoples, and places.

John continues, "I wept and wept because no one was found who was worthy to open the scroll...." (v. 4) He weeps because no one appears to be at the steering wheel of history guiding us to our destination. Think of all those deemed unworthy to rule: Krishna, Buddha, Muhammad, Darwin, Marx, Freud. None are worthy. No god. No guru. No philosopher. No scientist.

Then someone assures John, "'Do not weep! See, the Lion of the tribe of Judah... has triumphed. He is able to open the scroll and its seven seals.' Then I saw a Lamb, looking as if it had been slain..." (5:5-6).

We recognize this Lion-Lamb. He is Jesus!

John continues, "He came and took the scroll from the right hand of him who sat on the throne" (5:7). Thus God the Father places under Christ's rule and authority every moment of future history.

Now that Jesus holds this prize in His hand, what do you suppose He intends to do with history? ✏️▷

To understand Revelation 5, you only need to look at Matthew 28:18-19: "All authority in heaven and on earth has been given to me. Therefore go and make disciples of all nations...." Both texts describe the same event, but from different vantage points. Matthew 28:18-20 is the Great Commission from our earthly perspective. Revelation 5 is the Great Commission from God's heavenly perspective. Both affirm Jesus Christ is the Lord of every moment, including every second of our lives. Both reveal that the purpose of history and of our lives is to evangelize the lost.

Your role in history. After Jesus takes the scroll, the angels and twenty-four elders (including us) sing:

> You are worthy to take the scroll and to open its seals, because you were slain, and with your blood you purchased men for God from every tribe and language and people and nation. You have made them to be a kingdom and priests to serve our God, and they will reign on the earth (vv. 9-10).

During the first Holy Week, Christ had the opportunity to change history, and He did it! On the cross He purchased people from all over the globe. Triumphant over death, He is still directing history, transforming God's outreach prophecies and promises into reality. He does this through you and me, appointing us as His monarchs and priests to extend His gracious reign over every corner of the earth.

Every day you have opportunities to change history for people who are separated from God. Since your Savior has authority over all history, He also rules over the very moments when you witness. When you fear what may befall you if you speak about your Redeemer, recall who is the Ruler of that very moment.

How does this truth enable you to grasp your opportunities?
✐

Prayer: Jesus, I praise You that every tick of the clock is ruled by Your mighty hand.

Action: At the top of the pages in your daily or weekly planning calendar, regularly write: "You are worthy to take the scroll."

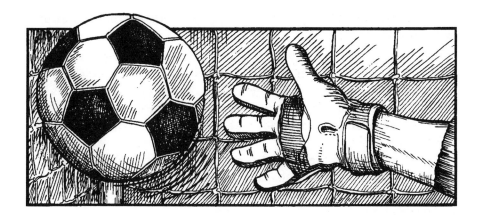

7 USING OUTREACH PROMISES

How many different ways can we put outreach promises to use? Will they make a significant impact on us as we carry out God's mission? This final chapter deals with these questions.

A. Sharers of the Good News

Hypothesis. In this book I have claimed that outreach promises will help you and all Christians to perform the following actions regularly, intentionally, happily, compassionately, confidently, zealously, and perseveringly.

- Witness about Christ the Savior to people lost without Him.
- Love, serve, and sacrifice for needy people in Christ's name.
- Enter new cultures and environments to share the faith.
- Plant churches among all people groups of the world.

In the medical world, it was not enough for some doctor to hypothesize that bee venom helps people with multiple sclerosis and other diseases. The hypothesis had to be tested in laboratories and with human beings. Data had to be gathered, cases analyzed, and research reports written.

You need to be just as scientific. Merely because someone claims outreach promises help Christians share their faith does not make it true. To test the validity of the hypothesis, you should experiment with outreach promises in your own witnessing situations.

Experiment. Here are ten basic guidelines for experimenting with outreach promises.

1. Understand your present setting and the people with whom you can share your faith. Revisit the "Clear objectives" section on pages 10-11. It contains questions to help you focus on your personal mission field. If you didn't answer the questions earlier, now is a good time to do so.

2. Identify the specific outreach doubts, fears, and discouragement which may be assailing you. You may find it helpful to review pages 11-16 where these terms are defined.

3. Remember evangelism is most enjoyable as a team sport. So whenever possible, work with other Christians who will reassure you and hold you accountable.

4. Find outreach promises which speak to your situation. Perhaps you have discovered some while reading this book. Others you will find as you read the Scriptures.

5. Focus on what God promises to do through you. Avoid turning outreach promises into commands, which would only add to your sense of inadequacy and guilt.

6. If you do find yourself trembling with outreach guilt, brace yourself with the grace found in gospel promises and rejoice.

7. Consciously, prayerfully apply your selected outreach promises to your doubts, fears, and disappointments. Fight these opponents with God's promises. Learn your favorite verses by heart for ready application.

8. Knowing and trusting outreach promises will help you obey God's outreach commands. So take action trusting God to keep His promises. Love, serve, and witness to others as God leads you.

9. Record what occurs. Is God faithful to His promises?

10. Note your development. As you continue to use outreach promises, do you sense progress in your willingness and ability to share your faith? What fruit is the Holy Spirit causing to grow?

This is where theory becomes reality. Put outreach promises to the test, and find out what the Lord will do for you through them.

Examples. The summer of 1997, I taught at a training seminar for thirty directors of evangelistic media offices on six continents. I encouraged them to find comfort in an amazing promise from Jesus: "I tell you the truth, anyone who has faith in me will do what I have been doing. He will do even greater things than these, because I am going to the Father" (Jn. 14:12).

I told the thirty media experts, "At first glance, this promise seems impossible. How can mere mortals do greater things than those performed by the Son of God when He walked this earth? But think about it. Jesus could preach to only several thousand people at one time. With radio, television, and web sites you are privileged to communicate God's word to millions all over the globe. This doesn't make us greater than Jesus, but God in His wisdom and power uses us to surpass what Jesus could accomplish in Israel in the first century. When your ministry becomes difficult—which may be often—embrace this promise."

To what personal situations might you apply Jesus' promise that "anyone who has faith in me.... will do even great things than these."? ▭

When my wife Julie was learning Spanish and adjusting to Venezuela—while at the same time caring for three preschoolers—she often found comfort in 2 Corinthians 4:16-18.

> Therefore, we do not lose heart. Though outwardly we are wasting away, yet inwardly we are being renewed day by day. For our light and momentary troubles are achieving for us an eternal glory that far outweighs them all. So we fix our eyes not on what is seen, but on what is unseen. For what is seen is temporary, but what is unseen is eternal.

Countless times Julie applied these words to her daily difficulties and thus found strength to persevere. Since then, we have met other missionary moms who said the Lord sustained them with the same outreach promise.

Prayer: Lord, I praise You for Your mighty word which both declares me righteous and empowers me to be Your witness.

Action: Purchase a notebook to record the data and findings of your outreach promise experiments.

B. Bible Rock Hounds

We have looked at many outreach promises, but hundreds more await our investigation! This little book has taught you Prospecting 101 and equipped you with a "gem detector" to identify words of outreach assurance and hope. Keep your eyes open for them whenever you read or listen to God's Word.

Amateurs. A friend of mine is an amateur geologist, but he prefers to call himself a rock hound. He vacations in places like Arizona, hiking through harsh terrain in search of metals and minerals to add to his collection.

Some readers of this book are like my rock hound friend. They are typical Christians with a moderate knowledge of the Bible. If that describes you, you may prefer to search for outreach promises with a friend or a Bible study group. That's great. The more people digging, the more gems you will find. To further whet your appetite, here are a few hints.

1. Outreach texts sometimes use the imagery of light and darkness. Examples: Is. 60:1-3; Mt. 5:14-16; Lk. 2:32; ans Jn. 8:12.

2. Outreach texts sometimes use the imagery of sowing, planting, and horticulture. Examples: Ps. 65; Ezek. 17:22-24; Mt. 13:1-43; Mk. 4:26-32; Jn. 15:1-17; & 1 Cor. 3:5-9.

3. Another common image is feasting, banquets, and celebration. Examples: Is. 25:6-9; Mt. 26:26-29; Lk. 14:1-24; Lk. 15; and Rev. 19:6-10.

4. You will find rich deposits of high grade ore in Isaiah, Revelation, and the Gospel of John, especially Jn. 14-17.

Experts. Other rock hounds prefer the professional title of "geologist." They have earned degrees in geology. Employed by oil firms and mining companies, they dig both deep and wide.

Readers of this book who are advanced Bible scholars resemble expert geologists. They delve into the Scriptures and theology. Some are college and seminary trained. Others are self-taught. If you are an advanced Bible scholar, you are aware this topic is much more complex than I have been able to portray in a thin, introductory volume. I invite you to study outreach promises in depth. Discuss the questions and issues with other scholars. On the basis of your discoveries, write theological papers about your discoveries, so that many may benefit from your efforts.

Here are some tantalizing puzzles you Bible experts might want to explore. I don't know the answers. I'm hoping you will teach me.

1. How many Old Testament outreach prophecies and promises are quoted in the New Testament? How are they used by the apostles and evangelists? What insights do we gain about how we should be using them? Begin your investigation with Acts 15:13-21, 2 Corinthians 6:14-7:1, and Galatians 3 (especially v. 8).

2. Some texts describe nature as praising God, for example, trees clapping their hands and fields being jubilant (Ps. 96:11-12; Ps. 98:7-9; Is. 44:23; Is. 55:12-13). Often such personifications of nature occur in a context of mission outreach. Why would this be? Is this merely poetry, or are the images pointing to something more literal? (See Rom. 8:19-22.)

3. Some Old Testament prophets received messages directed to nations nearby to Israel. Most of them are oracles of judgment, but some include positive elements, such as Isaiah 17, 18, and 19. Do we have any historical evidence whether these prophecies were ever sent to the nations or whether a nation ever responded?

Steps. Whether you are an amateur Bible rock hound or a professional one, you will enjoy discovering more outreach promises. To facilitate your search for outreach promises, consult Appendix 2: Maps of the Vein of Outreach Prophecy on pages 92-107.

What steps will you take to mine outreach promises.

✏️

Prayer: Holy Spirit, guide me as I search the Word for promises.

Action: Purchase a special-colored pen or highlighter with which to mark outreach promises in your Bible.

C. Pastors and Church Leaders

Do you long to see immobile Christians move out in pursuit of God's vision? Provide them steady doses of the Bible's good stings, outreach promises. Pastors and church leaders play a crucial role in this task.

See them and teach them. Picture Pastor Davis seated at his desk preparing a sermon on 2 Corinthians 1:3-11. He decides to emphasize verses 3-4:

> Praise be to the God and Father of our Lord Jesus Christ, the Father of compassion and the God of all comfort, who comforts us in all our troubles, so that we can comfort those in any trouble with the comfort we ourselves have received from God.

As Pastor Davis writes his sermon, he affirms how God comforts us amid troubles like illness, run-away children, and unemployment. Is this a legitimate application of the text? Since Paul says God "comforts us in *all* our troubles," it is appropriate. However, if Pastor Davis says no more than this, he will have overlooked the outreach promises in the text.

How?

The troubles which led Paul to pen these words were mission troubles. Opposed by Satan, pagans, and Jews who rejected their Messiah, Paul the Missionary writes:

> We do not want you to be uninformed, brothers, about the hardships we [missionaries] suffered in the province of Asia. We were under great pressure, far beyond our ability to endure, so that we despaired even of life. Indeed, in our hearts we felt the sentence of death (vv. 8-9).

Do you hear his anguish? Paul and his fellow missionaries weren't facing run-of-the-mill troubles and discomforts. They were suffering for the sake of spreading the gospel. "But this happened," Paul concludes, "that we might not rely on ourselves but on God, who raises the dead. He has delivered us from such a deadly peril, and he will deliver us" (vv. 9-10).

If Pastor Davis leaves Paul's mission intent on the cutting room floor, he will fail to motivate his people to share their faith on the basis of the outreach promises in 2 Corinthians 1:3-11.

Multiple uses. Pastors and church leaders can apply outreach promises in every setting where they communicate God's word.

a. Preaching. People tire of "you should" and "you ought." Energize them with "God will" and "God promises."
b. Worship and music. Find or create worship elements based on outreach promises. Begin with the music of Scott Wesley Brown. Take a new look at Psalm 67 and 100.
c. Prayer. God listens to petitions based on His promises.
d. Bible classes. Constantly identify the outreach promises in whatever scriptural text is being studied.
e. Visual arts. Use banners, paintings, windows, etc.
f. Bible memory. Make promises available for ready access.
g. Newsletters. Recruit volunteers in a positive manner.
h. Letters to missionaries. Pep up those on the front lines.

When I taught outreach promises to a pastors conference, many of them responded, "Now I have a way to promote evangelism and missions without hammering people with commands and orders." The pastors put their finger on why Christians need outreach promises. They don't load us of guilt. They fill us with faith, courage and confidence. God will establish in your church a climate of hopeful optimism, as you use outreach promises in your worship, Sunday school, youth work, evangelism, human care ministries, and missions.

Example. Dan Gilbert, co-pastor at Cross Lutheran Church in Yorkville, Illinois, says: "Awareness of outreach promises has changed our preaching and teaching. We frequently refer to the Lord's promises that His mission *will* be accomplished. We no longer quote the Great Commission without including its pre-promise and post-promise (Mt. 28:18, and 20b).

"Three years ago, we needed many fund-raising activities for my associate pastor and his wife to take a short-term mission trip. This year, I sent the church a letter stating that my wife and I were invited on a mission trip to Peru and Argentina. The expenses were covered in a couple weeks. Best of all, the prayer support exceeded the offerings. No fund-raisers. No bells and whistles. A single letter and Boom! How much of this is due to preaching the Word's outreach promises, I can't say, but the Holy Spirit is up to something here."

Steps. Whether you work on a church staff or are a lay person, what steps will you take to promote a steady dose of outreach promises in your church? ◉⊟▷

Prayer: Dear God, may Your outreach promises energize our worship, our love, our service, our witness, and all that we do.

Action: Take one of the steps you noted above.

D. Artists and Musicians

A favor. When my family and I lived in Mexico, my children were five, three, and two. One day as we walked down a sidewalk, we came to a driveway with wet cement. My three preschoolers came to a halt and gazed with longing at the freshly smoothed goo. To the workers watching from a distance, I yelled, "Don't worry, I won't let the children ruin your work."

But before I could shoo the kids away from the temptation, a young Mexican laborer ran up to us. Crouching down to the level of the children, he slapped a trowelful of wet cement on the sidewalk in front of them. Then he handed the trowel to the oldest child and chuckled, "Play!" For the next ten minutes, they took turns smoothing the cement flat and then piling it up again.

Returning the favor. I will never forget the wisdom and kindness of that young Mexican. I wrote this book to return his favor. Through the centuries, Christian artists and musicians have produced works based on messianic promises and end times promises. This book gives Christian artists a new load of cement to play with: outreach promises. If you are artistic, I hope you will have fun with it.

Your labors will encourage others. I often need encouragement myself. As I researched outreach promises for three years, I sometimes wondered if my efforts would bear any fruit. I was often uplifted by two works of art based on outreach promises.

First, above my desk is a calligraphy painting which my sister Susan designed for me when I graduated with a doctor of missiology degree. The painting features the earth and stars as seen from outer space. Spangled across the navy blue background are the words of Psalm 67:2: "Send us around the world with the news of your saving power and your eternal plan for all mankind" (*Living Bible*). I received a good sting every time I lifted my eyes to that cosmic scene and global promise.

Second, I often listened to a song with this chorus: "For the earth will be filled with the knowledge of the glory of the LORD, as the waters cover the sea" (Hab. 2:14). As the music crescendoed, my heart would swell with outreach hope. I know Habakkuk 2:14 sounds crazy, but our Savior God promised it! If He is crazy about saving the world, I want to be just as crazy. That song enabled me to maintain my intensity, and I'm sure it has helped many others. ("The Earth Shall Be Filled," by Ron Coile and David Morris, on *Worship the King*, Hosanna! Music)

The Sons of Korah. God may lead you to unite with others to produce art based on outreach promises. If you do, you'll be following the tradition of the Sons of Korah, who wrote several psalms. We know little about these fellows, but much of their portfolio emphasizes international outreach (See Ps. 44-49 & 87.).

When artists fail to develop the outreach themes in a text, a great opportunity is missed. For example, in 1779 John Newton penned the hymn "Glorious Things of Thee are Spoken, Zion, City of Our God." The title refers to Psalm 87:1-3, written by the Sons of Korah. While Newton's hymn describes heaven admirably, verses 4-6 of the psalm emphasize who will be there, a theme which Newton omits.

> I will record Rahab [Egypt] and Babylon among those who acknowledge me—Philistia too, and Tyre, along with Cush [the upper Nile region]— and will say, "This one was born in Zion."
>
> Indeed of Zion it will be said, "This one and that one were born in her, and the Most High himself will establish her." The Lord will write in the register of the peoples: "This one was born in Zion" (Ps. 87:4-6)

These are difficult verses to understand, but the outreach promise they contain is as magnificent as any found in the Bible. The countries listed were rivals and enemies of Israel. Contrary to typical nationalistic sentiments, the Sons of Korah urged the Jews to rejoice, because God would raise up believers even from among such nations. This Old Testament outreach prophecy is paralleled by the New Testament promise that the names of people from every tribe, language, people, and nation will be recorded in the Lamb's book of life (Rev. 7:9; 21:24-27).

In the 1980s, Wayne Watson wrote a song entitled, "Born in Zion" which is much closer to the meaning of Psalm 87 than John Newton's hymn. But even Watson failed to stress the multicultural, international nature of the promise expressed by the original lyricists, the Sons of Korah. Perhaps you or an artist friend of yours will accomplish that for the church.

Steps. If you are an artist or musician, or you know one, what steps will you take to develop works based on outreach promises? ◉⇨

Prayer: Lord, thank You for the arts. Help us apply them to Your outreach promises.

Action: Begin to take one of the steps you noted above.

E. It's Going to Happen!

What is the longest one-syllable word in the world?

It isn't "draughts" or even "straights." Every football (soccer) fan knows it is "Go-o-o-o-o-o-o-o-al!" At least it seems like "goal" is spelled that way when athletes, fans, and media announcers rejoice over a long-awaited score. Among world-class athletes, it is almost impossible to maneuver the ball past twelve attacking opponents and into the goal. Therefore, a team scores only when it executes its attack flawlessly. No wonder they go crazy.

"Go-o-o-o-o-o-o-o-al!" is the longest one-syllable word, because it celebrates the culmination of a hard-fought quest for perfection.

Three little words. One of the most cherished gospel promises is John's description of

> the Holy City, the new Jerusalem, coming down out of heaven from God, prepared as a bride beautifully dressed for her husband.... There will be no more death or mourn-

ing or crying or pain, for the old order of things has passed away" (Rev. 21:2, 4).

Following this comes Revelation 21:6. Take special note of the three little words in italics. "He said to me: '*It is done.* I am the Alpha and the Omega, the Beginning and the End. To him who is thirsty I will give to drink without cost from the spring of the water of life'."

Believe it or not, these three little words—"It is done"—comprise both the shortest and longest mission promise in the Bible. Shortest in number of letters. Longest in historical vision.

Three other words. Compare "It is done" to three other words. What did Jesus mean when He said, "It is finished" (Jn. 19:30)?

Every Christian believes that from the vantage point of the cross, Jesus saw all the sins of every person, claimed our wrongs as His own, and paid their penalty by His atoning blood. When Jesus declared "It is finished", He meant: "My work of redemption is completed. The prophecies about My once-for-all sacrifice are fulfilled." What a grand, consoling gospel promise!

Now let's return to "It is done."

A shout of triumph. Perhaps you have read Revelation 21 many times but hardly noticed "It is done." Now, may you marvel whenever you read those three little words, because in them God is shouting, "Go-o-o-o-o-o-o-o-al!"

Enthroned as ruler of the universe, presiding over the commencement of "a new heaven and a new earth," our Savior God declares "It is done!"

Read the words slowly. Savor them. He is announcing: "Human history, Part 1, is done. Though many rejected the gospel, it has been proclaimed as I desired. My rescue mission is now completed. All my outreach prophecies and promises are now thoroughly fulfilled."

Don't doubt the outcome for a second. Jesus promised, "This gospel of the kingdom will be preached in the whole world as a testimony to all the nations, and then the end will come" (Mt. 24:14). And that is exactly what will happen!

Don't fear the opposition of unbelievers or the dark powers of Satan. God is going to triumph!

Don't wallow in discouragement. Every outreach prophecy and promise is going to be fulfilled!

Sense the centuries. Use your imagination to meditate on Revelation 21:1-6. First, read the entire text from your Bible. Then close your eyes, and ask God to help you visualize in your mind the centuries of witnessing and cross-cultural expansion of the gospel summarized in those three little words, "It is done."

- Focus on continent after continent, city after city.
- See the preachers. See the everyday witnesses.
- See converts, bold to share their new faith.
- See the persecution. See the courage. See the martyrs.
- See yourself, playing your own one-person-sized role.

In all this grand enterprise directed by the Holy Spirit, what specifically do you picture yourself doing? Where and with whom are you serving? 🖎

I once taught the meaning of "It is done" in a Bible class. Near the close, a woman admitted with amazement, "Oh! It really *is* going to happen! I'm surprised and yet why should I be? All my life I've heard Bible verses about God's plan to proclaim Christ to every tribe, language, people, and nation. But, until now, it never had dawned on me that someday the task will actually be completed. What He promised, He will surely do."

Around AD 30, Jesus promised, "It is finished." When the present task of proclaiming liberation from sin, death, and Satan finally ends, God will declare, "It is done."

In between time, let us enjoy the adventure of getting it done.

Prayer: With all my heart, I trust Your words: "It is finished." With all my life, help me trust Your words: "It is done."

Action: With a friend share the "Sense the centuries" exercise above.

Where do we go from here?

AFTERWORD

This book is a basic introduction to outreach promises. I intend to keep studying them and writing about them. From time to time, I'll post this new material on my website. I hope you'll come and visit with me there.

URL: http://www.christianlink.com/evangelism/encourager

Help write the sequel. God willing, someday I may write an in-depth sequel. You, the readers of *Outreach Promises*, may write more of the sequel than I do, because it will report insights from:

a. Witnesses and missionaries who have trusted and acted upon outreach promises, proving their worth.
b. Bible students who have identified and studied hundreds of outreach promises.
c. Pastors and church leaders who have designed ways to share God's good stings in the life and worship of their churches.
d. Artists and musicians who have enhanced the beauty of God's gems for outreach encouragement.

Let's keep in touch. As you use outreach promises for all they are worth, you will make your own discoveries about them. So please keep me informed about what the Lord is teaching you through His outreach promises. I look forward to hearing from you. Choose the means of communication you prefer.

• E-mail: pmbickel@aol.com
• Address: 1167 Ryan Avenue W., Roseville, MN 55113-5929
• Phone: 651-487-1260

APPENDIX 1

GROUP DISCUSSION GUIDE

Setting and size. *Outreach Promises* can be discussed in groups of any size: Bible classes at church, small groups meeting in homes, evangelism and mission committees, as well as groups of men, women, and youth. The study lasts 7 or 8 sessions.

Goal and audiences. The goal is to encourage Christians to share their faith and support mission outreach. Participants may include folks who seldom witness, as well as people active in evangelism. All will benefit from outreach promises.

Leader's role. Formal teaching and lecturing are not required. The leader should seek an apprentice or co-leader. Duties include:

1. Recruit people to participate in the study.
2. Schedule meeting times and locations.
3. Assign a "host" to prepare refreshments.
4. Direct discussion, using the study guide for each chapter.
5. Establish an atmosphere of communication and caring.
6. Keep the conversations on track and moving along.
7. When possible, permit discussion in groups of about four.
8. Plan for learning to occur in the mind, spirit, and will.
9. Allow the Holy Spirit to direct the discussion.
10. Promote prayer both during sessions and between them.

Agenda and discussion. First, allow time for the group to gather and converse informally. Second, discuss the assigned chapter. Third, share prayer topics relating to Christian outreach, and then be sure to pray. Exactly how much time you devote to each of the three components will depend on your total time available. The following is a healthy balance: Gathering 10% of the available time; Discussion 60-70%; Prayer 20-30%.

Study Guide for Chapter 1:
Good Stings for Christian Outreach

Possible variations for starting the course:
If participants do not receive the book and read Ch. 1 ahead
of time, you may elect to devote two sessions to Ch. 1. If so, read
and discuss Sections A and B in class the first week. Then
assign Sections C, D, and E for the second session. In this case,
the course will last 8 sessions rather than 7.

Goals
1. To promote group cohesion and honest communication.
2. To value sharing the gospel with lost people.
3. To clarify one's present role(s) in witnessing and mission.
4. To identify outreach doubts, fears, and discouragement.
5. To begin to desire God's cure for our outreach paralysis.

Agenda
A. Informal conversation.
B. Discussion of Chapter 1.
1. Open with prayer.
2. Do you know people with multiple sclerosis or another
debilitating ailment? What might they think of a treatment which
relieved their symptoms?
3. In what ways do we experience outreach paralysis?
4. What remedy does the author propose? (See p. 8.)
5. What is your initial reaction to this proposed remedy?
6. Discuss the definitions in Section B. Determine your
group's level of understanding and agreement about these points.
7. In pairs, share responses to questions in Section B, Part 2.
8. Use questions in the text to discuss Sections C, D, & E.
C. Prayer.

Assignment
1. Either read Ch. 2 or read Ch. 1, Sections C, D, and E.
2. Respond to the discovery questions in the text.

Study Guide for Chapter 2:
Mining a New Vein of Prophecy

Goals
1. To promote group cohesion and honest communication.
2. To distinguish the three categories of prophecy.
3. To value the unique features of outreach prophecy.
4. To instill curiosity to mine the vein of outreach prophecy.
5. To desire to fulfill outreach prophecy, by the Spirit's power.

Agenda
A. Informal conversation.

B. Discussion of Chapter 2.

1. Open with prayer.

2. Has anyone here ever been inside a mine? What is it like?

3. Refer to the illustration on page 17. What does the author mean by this diagram?

4. Have you ever experienced the wonder of the messianic prophecies? What is your opinion of them?

5. Did you enjoy playing the Psalm 22 Game? What lessons did you learn by playing it?

6. To fulfill God's ongoing outreach prophecies is called an honor. Do you agree or disagree? Why?

7. How important is end times prophecy to you and your church?

8. Which of the three categories of prophecy is emphasized most in your church?

9. Are you eager to begin mining the Bible's vein of outreach prophecy? Why or why not?

10. At the end of each section of this chapter is a suggested "action step." Comment on an action you took.

C. Prayer.

Assignment
1. Read Chapter 3.
2. Respond to the discovery questions in the text.

Study Guide for Chapter 3:
Materials in the Vein of Outreach Prophecy

Goals

1. To promote group cohesion and open communication.
2. To distinguish commands and warnings from promises.
3. To overcome outreach guilt with gospel assurances.
4. To value the unique features of outreach promises.
5. To be able to identify outreach promises in Scripture.

Agenda

A. Informal conversation.

B. Discussion of Chapter 3.

1. Open with prayer.

2. Did you ever find something valuable by accident? Describe the experience.

3. For what purpose did God place outreach commands and warnings in the Bible? Why do we need to hear them?

4. How do you deal with guilt regarding your witnessing and mission deficiencies? How does God save us from a "cave-in"?

5. Review the discussion of Rom. 15:4-13 (pp. 32-33). Do you agree that Paul refers to and uses outreach promises in this text?

6. In Section D, which of the ten factors describing the value of outreach promises struck you as significant? Why?

7. What is meant by "Prospecting 101" in Section E?

8. Using the "prospecting" guidelines, can you identify other outreach promises? If so, what are they?

9. Do you agree that outreach promises serve a purpose distinctly different from outreach commands and warnings?

10. Are you eager to mine more promises? Why or why not?

11. Comment on an "action step" you took.

C. Prayer.

Assignment

1. Read Chapter 4.
2. Respond to the discovery questions in the text.

Study Guide for Chapter 4:
Outreach Promises and Sharing Your Faith

Goals

1. To strengthen group bonding and honest communication.
2. To allow Christ to teach us how to share our faith.
3. To replace pessimism with trust in the Holy Spirit's power.
4. To learn evangelism is done by God working through us.
5. To use positive self-talk and expect positive results.

Agenda

A. Informal conversation.

B. Discussion of Chapter 4.

    1. Open with prayer.

    2. How many like fishing? How many were taught how to fish? Is there a correlation between having had a teacher and liking to fish?

    3. Do you depend on Jesus to teach you to share your faith? Does it make a difference to do so? Why or why not?

    4. Do you know any churches or pre-Christians you consider hopeless cases? Do the promises in Section B apply to them?

    5. Review the story in Section C. Are you like an empty cup, a half-filled cup, a cup filled to the brim, or an overflowing cup? From whom does a Christian gain the ability to overflow?

    6. What kind of self-talk do you engage in regarding your ability to share God's truth with others? What difference would it make to tell yourself you have a spirit of power, of love, and of self-discipline? (See Section D and 2 Tim. 1:7-8.)

    7. When you face a witnessing opportunity, do you tend to think of worst-case scenarios or best-case scenarios?

    8. What hope do you garner from Peter's story in Section E?

    9. Comment on an "action step" you took.

C. Prayer.

Assignment

1. Read Chapter 5.
2. Respond to the discovery questions in the text.

Study Guide for Chapter 5:
Outreach Promises and Mission Work

Goals
1. To promote group bonding and honest sharing.
2. To instill hopefulness that mission work is possible.
3. To overcome cultural obstacles to mission work.
4. To trust God's promises for serving in all environments.

Agenda
A. Informal conversation.

B. Discussion of Chapter 5.

1. Open with prayer.

2. Do you know any missionaries? What is their life and ministry like? Do you ever think of yourself as a missionary?

3. Is it realistic to view foreigners and strangers as your not-yet brothers and not-yet sisters? Why, or why not?

4. What multicultural tensions do you face? Do the promises in Section B provide you sufficient hope to cope?

5. Define cross-cultural and cross-environmental ministry.

6. What cross-cultural or cross-environmental opportunities present themselves to you? What outreach promises motivate you to serve in these challenging fields?

7. Are you ready and willing to be God's mobile temple? What is your court of the Gentiles? Your church's court of the Gentiles? What obstacles or distractions might Christ need to clear away?

8. Discuss responses to the list of challenges in Section E.

9. Consider the ten promises in Section E. How difficult would mission work be without God's promises of fruitfulness? How much easier is the task with them?

10. Comment on an "action step" you took.

C. Prayer.

Assignment
1. Read Chapter 6.
2. Respond to the discovery questions in the text.

Study Guide for Chapter 6:
Facing Obstacles and Opponents

Goals

1. To increase group honesty and cohesion.
2. To candidly face the difficulties of Christian outreach.
3. To rejoice that God is aware of and equal to the difficulties.
4. To learn to trust God in the midst of turmoil and troubles.

Agenda

A. Informal conversation.

B. Discussion of Chapter 6.

1. Open with prayer.

2. Have you ever volunteered for a job that was more than you bargained for? Describe the experience.

3. God matches every difficulty we will face with a promise. Are you satisfied with this assurance? Is it enough? Why, or why not?

4. Discuss this opinion: Even the verses in which God honestly portrays outreach difficulties are also outreach promises.

5. Which translation of Matthew 16:18 do you prefer? Why?

6. Are the keys of the kingdom substantial enough weapons with which to oppose Satan, demons, and unbelievers? What other spiritual weapons does the Lord provide us?

7. Discuss the story in Mark 4:35-5:20, scene by scene. Share your responses to the discovery questions in Section C.

8. Does viewing outreach promises as prayer catalysts change how you pray? What promises attract your attention?

9. Review Revelation 5 (Section E). Do you agree this scene is Matthew 28:18-20 from the perspective of heaven? What difference does it make that Christ is the Ruler of every moment?

10. Comment on an "action step" you took.

C. Prayer.

Assignment

1. Read Chapter 7.
2. Respond to the discovery questions in the text.

Study Guide for Chapter 7:
Using Outreach Promises

Goals
1. To discuss ways to develop and use outreach promises.
2. To design personal strategies for using outreach promises.
3. To design team strategies for using outreach promises.
4. To resolve, with God's help, to implement our strategies.

Agenda
A. Informal conversation.

B. Discussion of Chapter 7.

1. Open with prayer.

2. Through what steps must a theoretical medical cure proceed before it can be considered a safe and reliable remedy?

3. Review the ten steps for experiments in Section A? Are you willing to follow them? Why or why not? What might occur if you were to do so with some other Christians? (See Jn. 14:12-14.)

4. In regard to Bible knowledge, do you consider yourself more like an amateur rock hound or a professional geologist? What steps will you take to mine outreach promises?

5. Brainstorm ways to use outreach promises in your church.

6. What steps will you take to provide a steady dose of good stings in your church?

7. "A picture is worth a thousand words." Does this maxim hold true with artistic renditions of outreach promises? Give examples.

8. Whether you are an artist or not, what steps will you take to develop works based on outreach promises?

9. How much do you cherish the promise "It is finished"? How much do you cherish the promise "It is done"?

10. Do the visualizing exercise "What you see" in Section E. Share responses to the discovery questions there.

11. Design personal and group strategies to use outreach promises. Don't skim over this. It is the key to the future. You may even decide to continue meeting to pursue this goal further.

C. Prayer.

APPENDIX 2

MAPS OF THE VEIN OF OUTREACH PROPHECY

You might think a book on outreach promises should list them all. But that would spoil the fun of finding them yourself.

My mining adventure. In his book *In the Gap* David Bryant proposes a method to help Christians see the world as God sees it. Bryant advises: (1) buy a new Bible; (2) read it in its entirety with the purpose of identifying everything related in any way to evangelism and missions; and (3) mark all the appropriate texts with a distinctively colored pen or highlighter.

When I read about this idea in 1979, it aroused my wanderlust. But, exhibiting amazing powers of procrastination, I put it off for an entire decade. Finally, in 1990, I purchased a red pen and a large-print Bible for the relief of my on-the-threshhold-of-bifocals eyes.

Before long my Bible had turned red. What a mind-expanding experience! God's concern for the whole world is not merely an occasional theme of Scripture. It's the very heartbeat of the Bible. All the world is in all the Word.

Every section I marked in red was part of the Bible's vein of outreach prophecy. Over the years, I continued to dig in this vein and discovered the materials the Lord placed there: outreach commands; outreach warnings; and those marvelous gems of encouragement, outreach promises

Maps. Miners are always glad to have maps of the subterranean deposits they seek to unearth. That is what this appendix is—maps of the vein of outreach prophecy. Consulting these charts will give you an idea of what to expect in each book of the Bible. Read the books in any order you like. As you make "Aha!" discoveries along the way, add your own notes to the maps.

If you are the kind of person who prefers to make discoveries on your own, don't consult my notes until after you have read a portion of Scripture. In this way you'll have both the satisfaction of finding the treasures yourself, plus the encouragement of comparing your findings with mine.

Before you begin, here are two more pieces of advice.

All-inclusive landmarks. Remember, mining the vein of outreach prophecy is more than simply prospecting for paraphrases of the Great Commission. Often God communicates his concern for the lost through very simple, but all-inclusive terms, such as: all, the world, the earth, man, men, person, nations, tribes, families, Jews and Gentiles, many, us, you, he who, whoever, no one, anyone, and everyone.

In addition to all-inclusive terms, the Bible has many all-inclusive teachings, doctrines which apply to both your neighbors and the nations. These include: creation, sin, forgiveness of sin, redemption, faith and unbelief, new life in Christ, death and resurrection, heaven and hell, etc.

All-inclusive terms and all-inclusive teachings are your basic navigational landmarks to guide you through the Bible's vein of outreach prophecy. May the Holy Spirit cause them to jump off the page and grab your heart, compelling you to see both your lost neighbors and the billions in unreached people groups.

Staying on course. How can you stay focused on outreach themes while reading the Bible? How can you remain focused during your prayer time which often follows Scripture reading?

Use verbal aids to help you stay focused. The following categories of people express the full scope of the Bible's message.

- Religions of the world
- Continents, regions, and islands
- Nations of the world
- Ethnic people groups of the world
- Language groups of the world
- Religious and ethnic groups in your own community

To learn how to use these categories, try this little exercise. Consider John 3:36: "Whoever believes in the Son has eternal life, but whoever rejects the Son will not see life, for God's wrath remains on him." Meditate on the verse, substituting items from

the six categories above in place of the words "whoever" and
"him" in John 3:36. For example: Muslims from the Maldive
Islands, believing in the Son will have eternal life. As you do so,
you will see truths in the text which escaped you before.

Also try visual aids. Have you ever read your Bible with a
world map or atlas opened before you? Just glancing at the maps
reminds you that God's Word is intended for those who live in
distant places. Use pictures of people from other cultures to
keep you thinking globally. Take a *National Geographic* and cut
out pictures of folks from around the world. Mix them together
to make your own collage of faces for whom Christ bled and died.

GENESIS

The Creation and Fall narratives are foundational for all mission
work and strategy. From ch. 4 on, "nation" is a key word. God founds all
the nations, not just Israel. Abraham, Isaac, and Jacob are repeatedly
promised their descendants will be a great nation, in order that all peoples
may be blessed through them.

Judgment on nations: the Flood, Tower of Babel, Sodom and Gomorrah.

Gen. 49:10 The Man of Peace whom the nations will obey.

EXODUS

Theme: that nations know the Lord. Israel (14:31), Egypt (5:2), and
others (9:16).

The plagues are warfare against the gods of Egypt (18:11).

The covenant given at Sinai calls them to serve only one God.

Ex. 19:4-6 says Israel will be a kingdom of priests and a holy nation.

Judgment on the nations in Canaan.

"For coming generations" is a repeated theme in Tabernacle plans.

Israel's glory is God's presence (Shekinah), 33:15-16 and 40:34-38.

LEVITICUS

Animists seek to influence gods and spirits by their sacrifices. In
contrast, God granted the Jews mercy and atonement through his sacrificial system. Due to the Passover, the Lord already owned the first
born. Therefore, no fertility sacrifices were permitted.

Ch. 1-15 have very little on evangelism and mission. Ch. 16-27 are a
call to fulfill Ex. 19:6: (a) to be a holy nation; (b) to avoid the pagan sins
of the Canaanites; (c) to treat the aliens kindly; and (d) to worship no
other gods. Their holiness will be a witness to the nations. Ch. 20:26.

NUMBERS

Very little on evangelism and mission in ch. 1-10.

Ch. 11 Universal outpouring of the Holy Spirit is desired.

Allegorical parallels to mission: (a) Israel had the resources, as the
censuses show, just as the Church today is capable of completing the

Great Commission; (b) they refused to enter and take the land, just as many generations of Christians have failed to take the Great Commission seriously; (c) the Trans-Jordan tribes committed to complete the conquest, just as those who now have the gospel ought not grow complacent.

Ch. 22-25 Midian and Balaam; no pagan, occult curse works against Israel (Gen. 12:3).

The closing chapters show how Israel brought judgment on the nations. We are called to bring them life.

Look for references to "the alien."

Global statements: 14:21; 16:22; 27:16.

> Then all the peoples of the earth will see that you are called by the name of the LORD.
> Dt. 28:10

DEUTERONOMY

Allegorical parallel between conquest of Canaan and world evangelization.

Judgment on the nations.

Mention of nations round about and YHWH's sovereignty over them.

The Law was to attract the nations by its justice and holiness. Obedience will put Israel above them. Ch. 18 denounces all spiritism as well as prophesying about the Great Prophet to come.

YHWH the only God. Destroy and avoid counterfeits of the nations.

If Israel disobeys, God will use other nations to punish them.

Several references to the duty of teaching the next generation.

Refrain in the Law: "the fatherless, the alien and the widow."

Ch. 30 parallels Rom. 10. Ch. 31 parallels the Great Commission.

JOSHUA

Gods' judgment on evil, idolatrous nations. Only Rahab, her family, and the Gibeonites are spared.

Mission parallels are found in: (a) Ch. 7, Achan's sin halts the mission; (b) Ch. 14, 15, Caleb's eager bravery; (c) Ch. 17, Ephraim's and Manasseh's need to expand their territory; (d) Ch. 18, charting the final division; and (5) Ch. 22, the Eastern tribes fulfilling the mission that Moses and God gave them.

Ch. 23-24 Joshua preaches for revival, a people movement in Israel.

JUDGES

Idolatry, syncretism, and war against oppressing nations.

Ch. 6 Power encounter between Gideon and Baal.

RUTH

A foreigner is drawn into Israel and the lineage of the Messiah.

1 SAMUEL

Ch. 5 The Ark in the Temple of Dagon shows supremacy of Yahweh.

Samuel repeatedly calls Israel to turn from idolatry and syncretism.

Hebrews demand a king, like the nations.

Ch. 15 Saul fails to fulfill his mission against the Amalekites.

Ch. 17 David's "power encounter" against Goliath.

David and Saul clash, amidst wars against Philistines and others.
Ch. 28 Saul sinks to occult practices.

2 SAMUEL

Many battles against enemies, especially the Philistines.
Ch. 7 Promise to David of eternal kingdom; note vv. 22-26.
Ch. 11 Sin against Uriah the Hittite.
Ch. 15 Ittai the Gittite follows David in his darkest hour.
Ch. 21 The Gibeonites revenged.
Ch. 22-23 Songs of David regarding his rule over the nations.

1 KINGS

Solomon: (a) his worldwide renown and sharing of God's revelation; (b) his prayer at the dedication of the temple contains great O.T. mission theology; (c) his demise and idolatry.

The rest of 1 Kings speaks of the kings who either promoted idolatry or fought against it. Ahab stands out as the worst.
Ch. 18 Elijah and the prophets of Baal.
Ch. 20 God of both the mountains and the plains.
Ch. 22 Micaiah and the false prophets.

2 KINGS

Ch. 1 Ahab consults Baal-Zebub in Moab.
Ch. 5 Naaman of Aram.
Ch. 6 Elisha traps blinded Arameans.
Ch. 9-10 Jehu avenges Ahab and Jezebel.
Ch. 17 Assyria conquers and deports Israel.
Ch. 18-19 God defeats Assyria at Jerusalem.
Ch. 21 Manasseh's idolatry.
Ch. 22-23 Josiah's revival.
Ch. 24-25 Judah deported to Babylon.

> ...for men will hear of your great name and your outstreched arm.
> 1 Kings 6:42

1 CHRONICLES

Ch. 1 The Nations; descendants of Adam.
Wars against Philistines and other nations.
The reign of David and expansion of his kingdom: a type of the expansion of Messiah's Kingdom. Ch. 14:17
Ch. 16:7-36 David's psalm of thanks is global in emphasis.
Ch. 17 Eternal reign of Messiah predicted by God.
Ch. 28-29 David's preparations to build temple and offerings given by Israel. We should be no less dedicated to building the N.T. Temple—the people of God from among all nations (Is. 56:6-8).

2 CHRONICLES

Constant struggle between the worship of Yahweh and idolatry.
Reforms, renewal of covenant, and revival of faith. All three steps (27:2-3) are needed to restore them to God.
Ch. 2 Temple built with help of many foreigners.
Ch. 6:32-33 The foreigner who seeks God.

Ch. 7:14, 19-22 If my people obey, or follow idols....

Ch. 9 Wisdom of Solomon, Queen of Sheba and others.

Ch. 14-16 Asa's reforms, victories and failures. 16:9.

Ch. 17-20 Jehoshaphat's reforms and attempted revival. 19:4-7, 20:33.

Ch. 23 Joash, reform followed by idolatry.

Ch. 25:7-8 God is no longer with Israel.

Ch. 25:14-24 Amaziah beguiled by Edom's gods.

Ch. 28 Idolatry of Ahaz.

Ch. 30:1-31:1 Hezekiah's Passover, reform, apparent revival.

Ch. 32 Sennacherib - battle of the Gods.

Ch. 33 Manasseh promotes idolatry, and then reform.

Ch. 34 Josiah's reforms, covenant and apparent revival.

Ch. 35:21 Neco, King of Egypt, claims a revelation from God.

Ch. 36 Jerusalem destroyed due to idolatry. V. 23 Cyrus appears to have faith in Yahweh.

EZRA

Ch. 1 God moves the heart of King Cyrus.

Ch. 5-6 God moves the heart of King Darius.

Ch. 8 God moves heart of King Artaxerxes to send Ezra to Jerusalem.

Ch. 9-10 God moves hearts of those who intermarried with unbelievers.

NEHEMIAH

Ch. 2 God turns the heart of King Artaxerxes.

Ch. 8-10 A people movement back to Yahweh.

Ch. 13 Halting of marriage to foreigners.

ESTHER

An example of hatred toward God's people.

An example of how God quietly works among the nations.

JOB

Satan opposes the godly all over the world. 1:7-8, 2:2-3.

Job's experiences had an impact on the whole world, or at least the East (1:3).

The dialog centers on universal themes: the evil of humankind; the certainty of death; and the justice of God before human evil

God's authority to rule (as Creator) and his willingness to forgive the truly repentant, are also stressed.

Ch. 28 Poem about wisdom and revelation which come from God alone.

PSALMS

The many evangelism and mission themes of Psalms are summarized below.

Messiah is to rule the nations: 2, 18, 22, 72, 89, 110.

The witness of a righteous ruler: 101.

God rules the earth: 8, 11, 24, 33, 46, 49, 60, 68, 76, 108, 113, 146.

All nations will see and hear: 22; 45:12, 17, 47, 48, 57, 65, 66, 67, 72, 86, 87, 97, 98, 99, 113, 117, 138, 148, 150:6.

Judgment of the wicked and the righteous: 1, 5, 7, 9, 10, 12, 21, 31, 37, 49, 50, 55, 58:11, 59, 64, 75, 92, 94, 96, 110.

Forgiveness, mercy, and salvation: 32, 36:7-9, 51, 85, 130, 145.

Proclaim, tell: 9, 35:28, 40, 57:9, 66, 71, 78, 89:1-2, 96, 108, 116, 117, 145, 148, 149, 150.

People as lost sinners: 14, 36:1-2, 37, 39, 51:5, 53, 89, 47-8, 90, 143:2.

Idolatry, and the contrasting uniqueness of Yahweh: 4, 77:13-15, 81, 82, 86, 89:6-8, 93, 97, 106, 115, 135.

Creation of the world: 8, 95, 100, 104, 121:2, 124:8, 134:3, 136, 139.

Creation of the human race: 8, 62:9-10, 139.

God's revelation to the world: 19, 97, 147.

Unity of the Church: 133.

Victory viewed as a witness to nations: 44, 60, 79, 80, 83, 89, 102, 105, 114, 126, 136, 137, 144.

Persecution for sake of God's Kingdom: 44.

> The LORD reigns, let the earth be glad; let the distant shores rejoice. Ps. 97:1

PROVERBS

Countless themes in Proverbs are related to evangelism and missions: life and death; wisdom and folly; righteous and wicked, the sinfulness of people; lips, witness, and messenger; tree of life and fountain of life; God's sovereignty over all people; his knowledge of everyone's heart; his ability to judge human evil; salvation as God's doing only; God as Creator of both rich and poor, care for the poor; passing on a right fear of God to children; sluggards and the Great Commission; future hope for the righteous; and the error of trusting in one's own righteousness, wisdom, ideas, wealth, and power.

Ch. 8-9 The public invitation of wisdom and folly to all people.

Significant verses: 11:30; 21:30; 24:11-12; 25:25-26; 28:9-13.

ECCLESIASTES

Many peoples of the world can relate to this dirge about death and the meaninglessness. The writer tries many approaches to life, and still feels it lacks any meaning, except to simply accept and enjoy it.

Ch. 3:10-11 Eternity in their hearts.

Ch. 7:20, 29; 9:3 Universal sinfulness.

Ch. 8:17 Unable to uncover the truth of life and God.

Ch. 12 Remember your Creator in the days of your youth.

SONG OF SONGS

Allegorically speaking, believers in Christ are both the Beloved and the Friends, introducing people from all lands to the One who can fill their hearts, souls and minds with a passionate love, such as that described here. One's relationship with God is to be passionate, personal, and free of interlopers.

ISAIAH

Isaiah is not only the Evangelist of the O.T., but also the Apostle of the O.T. An overarching global emphasis is found throughout the book. The following list doesn't begin to note all the details.

Ch.1-12 The Jews are called to be a light to the nations, but they share in the false religions around them.

Ch. 2, 9, 11, 12. Messianic promises are related to the nations.

Ch. 13-23 Prophecies about the nations demonstrate Yahweh's sovereignty over the nations and his opposition to idolatry, occult practices, and universalism. Especially noteworthy are the prophecies about Cush in ch. 18 and Egypt in ch. 19.

Ch. 24-35 Calls to worship Yahweh alone.

Ch. 25 Yahweh will conquer death for all nations.

Ch. 36-39 Defeat of Assyria shows nations the Lord is the only God.

Ch. 40-66 Yahweh often proclaims his divinity and uniqueness, referring to his work of creation, revelation, and salvation, in contrast to the inactivity of the idols. The Servant Songs could also be called the Servant of the Nations Songs.

Ch. 56 Citizenship in the O.T. Kingdom is expanded.

Ch. 61:11 Conclusion of the text Jesus read at Nazareth.

Ch. 66 Conclusion with many global themes. Vv. 18-21 foretell the spread of the Gospel after Christ gives the Great Commission.

JEREMIAH

Themes related to mission: idolatry, destruction by Babylon and resultant infamy among the nations, wiles of false prophets, and persecution of Jeremiah.

Ch. 1:5 Called to be a prophet to the nations.

Ch. 4:1-2 The nations are to be blessed by Israel's faithfulness.

Ch. 7 False hope in the Temple (syncretism).

Ch. 9 Unfaithfulness of the circumcised.

Ch. 10 God and idols.

Ch. 12:16 Other nations are called to follow Yahweh.

Ch. 13 Linen belt, God's honor is bound to his people.

Ch. 16:19-21 Other nations are called to follow Yahweh.

Ch. 18 If a nation obeys; and if not.

Ch. 25 Cup of wrath and list of kings.

Ch. 29 Advice for life in the foreign land of Babylon.

Ch. 32:20 God's signs among all humankind.

Ch. 33 The nations will be affected by the New Covenant.

Ch. 38-39 Ebed-Melech the Cushite.

Ch. 44 Refugees in Egypt worship the Queen of Heaven.

Ch. 46-51 Oracles against nations and their gods; especially Babylon.

LAMENTATIONS

A hymn of repentance for failing to glorify God among the nations. Even when the nations gloat over the fall of Jerusalem, still the Lord reigns and is capable of redeeming and restoring his people to a blessed relationship with Him.

EZEKIEL

Recurrent phrase: "Then they will know that I am the Lord."
Ch. 18 The soul that sins will die. No pleasure in death of wicked.
Ch. 20 Return from exile will occur "for my name's sake".
Ch. 22:30 The need for someone to stand in the gap.
Ch. 27-28 Prophecy about Tyre and its commerce.
Ch. 29 Egypt will become lowly kingdom.
Ch. 32 The realm of the dead.
Ch. 33 Parable of the Watchman.
Ch. 34 The Shepherd who will protect Israel from the nations.
Ch. 36 Link between obedience and nations knowing Yahweh is Lord.
Ch. 37 One nation, one King.
Ch. 38-39 Gog and Magog.
Ch. 47 The land is given to aliens too.

> Now I, Nebuchadnezzar, praise and exalt and glorify the king of heaven.
> Dan. 4:37

DANIEL

Even though Judah has been defeated, Yahweh rules over the nations and rulers.

Prophetic dreams and visions testify that, even though nations rise and wane, Yahweh will establish an everlasting global kingdom ruled by the Coming King, described as the Rock not cut by human hands (2:44-45), the One like a Son of Man (7:13-27) and the Anointed One (9:20-27).

Ch. 12:1-4 Universal resurrection and judgment.

HOSEA

Hosea speaks exclusively of the relationship of Yahweh to Israel and Judah. He uses powerful imagery, especially regarding adultery (Ch. 1, 3, 14). However, the N.T. application of "Not loved" and "Not my people" (1 Peter 2:9-10), shows that what Hosea says about Israel and Judah pertains to all nations.

JOEL

Army of locusts (like the Egyptian plague) resembles the Last Day.
Ch. 2:27-32 The Spirit of God poured out on all. See Acts 2.
Ch. 3 Nations judg in Valley of Jehoshaphat, Jerusalem secure.

AMOS

God judges the sins of all nations. Israel is singled out here. Although worshiping Yahweh outwardly, their idolatry and syncretism are evident, along with their oppression of the poor and needy while they lounge in their mansions.

Ch. 8:11-14 Famine of the word of Yahweh; death of idolaters.

Ch. 9 Although Israel will be sifted, David's tent will be restored so that they may possess all the nations that bear God's name. See Acts 15.

OBADIAH

Despite Jerusalem's defeat, the kingdom is the Lord's (21). He will punish Edom and all wicked nations and provide salvation through Mt. Zion (Jn. 4:22).

JONAH

What in this story is not missionary in nature? Read it as though you were a member of a people like the Ninevites, who had never heard the word of God. Ch. 4:11 A call to urban mission.

MICAH

Ch. 4-5 Global proclamation of God's reign through the Messiah.
Ch. 3 False prophets and the Spirit of the Lord.
Ch. 7:18 Uniqueness of God's mercy. Proclaim this to the nations.

NAHUM

God rules over powerful, vicious nations like Assyria, condemning their idolatry and sorcery (1:14, 2:4). Also God's judgment on Egypt.

HABAKKUK

An evil nation, Babylon, will conquer Judah (not quite as evil). Ultimately, God will punish the evil of both nations. Trust in God's eventual retribution (3:16-19), as well as his eventual triumph in all the earth (2:13-14).

ZEPHANIAH

God's judgment on all nations and on the unfaithfulness of Judah.
Ch. 3:9-10, 20 Hope offered to all the nations who call on his name.

HAGGAI

Ch. 2:7 "... the desired of all nations will come..."
Ch. 3:21-23 A similar promise to Zerubbabel, "my signet ring."
Preaching about building temple includes the nations. So should ours today: re. church buildings and the spiritual temple of the Church.

ZECHARIAH

There are abundant references to the nations turning to the Lord.
Ch. 1 God's angels range throughout the world.
Ch. 4:6 "Not by might, nor by power, but by my Spirit."
Ch. 9 The King on a donkey will proclaim peace to the nations.
Ch. 14 Nations war against Jerusalem; celebrate Feast of Tabernacles.
Preaching about building temple includes the nations. So should ours today: re. church buildings and the spiritual temple of the Church.

MALACHI

The Lord is coming. All nations will serve the Lord. The Lord will distinguish the faithful from the faithless (not along national or ethnic lines). Faulty offerings short circuit God's plan to bless us and the nations.

MATTHEW

This most Jewish of the Gospels contains many mission emphases.

Ch. 1 Note the Gentiles in Jesus' ancestry.

Ch. 2 The Magi from the East.

Ch. 4 Temptation includes all kingdoms; Galilee of the Gentiles.

Ch. 5-7 Sermon on Mt., guidelines for world Christians (5:1-16, 7:7-14).

Ch. 8 Feast with Abraham, Isaac, and Jacob; Gadarene demoniac.

Ch. 9:35-38 Prayer for harvest workers.

Ch. 10 Instruction to disciples on their first evangelistic mission.

Ch. 12:18-21 See Is. 42:1-4.

Ch. 13:38 Teaching through parables; the field is the world.

Ch. 15:21-28 The Canaanite woman.

Ch. 16:18-19; 18:18 Loosing and binding on earth.

Ch. 16:24ff Take up your cross and follow me.

Ch. 17:20 Compare to Zech. 4:6-7.

Ch. 18 Meaning of discipleship; faith of little children; reclaim lost sheep.

Ch. 19:16-30 Forsaking things for Christ is what missionaries do.

Ch. 20-21 Workers in the vineyard; parable of tenants.

Ch. 22 Parable of wedding banquet; taxes to Caesar; two commands.

Ch. 23 Law preached to moral, religious unbelievers.

Ch. 24-25. End times, Christ's coming, and global outreach (24:14).

Ch. 26:3 Wherever the Gospel will be announced.

Ch. 26:27-28 Lord's Supper, "poured out for many".

Ch. 26:69ff Peter fails to be a witness.

Ch. 27 Crucifixion; v. 32 Simon of Cyrene; v. 54 Roman Centurion.

Ch. 28:18-20 The Great Commission.

MARK

Jesus draws attention of both Jews and Gentiles, individuals and populaces. Constantly calling people to believe and to share his message, then sending them.

Many of the parables speak of spreading his word.

Ch. 5:1-20 Satanic opposition; Jesus triumphs; missionary to Decapolis.

Ch. 11 A House of prayer for all nations (Is.56:7).

Ch. 12:29-34 The man not far from the kingdom of God.

All 3 times that he predicts his death, he calls them to servanthood.

Ch. 15 Simon of Cyrene; the Centurion.

Ch. 16:9-20 Summary of basic outreach themes of this gospel.

LUKE

Outreach is central to life and mission of Jesus, from the dedication to Theophilus (probably a Gentile), to the closing reference to Old Testament mission prophecies.

People Jesus reached:

Ch.1:46ff Mary.

Ch. 2:10, 11, 17 Shepherds.

Ch. 2:29-32, 38 Simeon and Anna.

Ch. 5:10 Disciples (fishers of men).

Ch. 5:27-32 Levi and friends.

Ch. 6:17 Crowds of Gentiles.
Ch. 7:1-10 The centurion.
Ch. 8:22-39 The demoniac.
Ch. 17:11-19 Ten lepers.
Ch. 18:18ff Rich Young Ruler.
Ch. 19:1-10 Zacchaeus.
Ch. 23:1-43 Thief on the Cross.
Ch. 23:26 Simon of Cyrene.

> ... knock and
> the door will be
> opened to you.
> Luke 11:9

Parables and preaching regarding outreach:
Ch. 4 Sermon in Nazareth with Gentile examples.
Ch. 6:7ff Sermon on the Plain.
Ch. 8:5-18 Parable of sower; of lamp.
Ch. 10:25ff The good Samaritan.
Ch. 11 Prayer, strong man, Jonah and Queen of Sheba.
Ch. 12 Rich fool, seek kingdom, not peace but division.
Ch. 13 Mustard seed, narrow door, feast.
Ch. 14 Banquet teachings, cost of discipleship.
Ch. 15 Lost sheep, coin, and son. Note the joy!
Ch. 16:19-31 Rich man and Lazarus.
Ch. 19:11-27 Parable of 10 minas.
Ch. 20 Parable of tenants, Caesar.
Ch. 21 End times, preaching to nations.
Ch. 22:19-20 Lord's Supper.
Ch. 24:44-49 Worldwide mission foretold.

Training and sending:
Ch. 3:4-6 John the Baptist quotes Isaiah.
Ch. 5:10 Fishers of men.
Ch. 9 Sending of the 12.
Ch. 10 Sending of the 72.
Ch. 9:51-6 A Samaritan village. See Acts 8:1-25.

Other:
Ch.3:21ff Christ's genealogy goes to Adam.
Ch. 4 Temptation (concerning the nations).
Ch. 23:38 King of the Jew.

JOHN

Throughout this Gospel, Jesus focuses his ministry on lost people. Many individuals meet Jesus. The issue is: Will they believe in him or not?

Below are listed many mission terms and themes which appear in John so often that all the references cannot be cited.

World (The "I am's" are global.).
Send (The Father sent the Son; he now sends us).
Eternal life.
Believe, faith.
Judgment.
Devil, thief, prince of this world.
Judaism, the Christ, rejection of their King.

Divinity of Christ: the Father's missionary to the world.

The need to honor the Son and the Father. All must respond.

Ch. 14-17 Mission is the theme of this discourse. Note the repetition of words like Spirit, fruit, prayer, world, love, glory, persecution, and unity.

ACTS

The story of the apostolic, that is, missionary church. Limit underlining to the verses you consider most outstanding.

Ch. 1-7 The Word of the Lord grows in Jerusalem.

Ch. 1:8 Great Commission as stated in Acts, an outline of the book.

Ch. 8-12 The Word of the Lord grows in the eastern Mediterranean.

Ch. 13-15 Paul's first journey; Council at Jerusalem on mission issues.

Ch. 16-18:22 Paul's second missionary journey.

Ch. 18:23-21:16 Paul's thirdmissionary journey.

Ch. 21:21-26:32 Paul's arrest in Jerusalem; his witness in prison.

Ch. 27-28 Paul's voyage to Roman and witness in that city.

ROMANS

Romans brims with insights re. the Church's global mission. For more on the missiological view of Romans, consult *The Goal of the Gospel*, by Philip M. Bickel and Robert L. Nordlie (See page 111.).

Ch. 1:5 Summary of church's mission. Compare 1:1-7 to 16:25-27.

Ch. 1:16 Jews + Gentiles = all people; repeated throughout letter.

Ch. 1:18-3:20 Guilt and lostness of all; need of a universal Savior.

Ch. 3:21-5:21 Work of the universal Savior. Note ch 4:12, 13, 17.

Ch. 8:28-39 Paul's commentary on Mt. 28:20b.

Ch. 9-11. Questions of how the lost can receive God's mercy.

Ch. 12:1-2 Paul's alter [not a typo] call: Become world Christians.

Ch. 13:1-7 Love legal authorities even when they oppose evangelism.

Ch. 14 Ethical debates between believers from different ethnic groups.

Ch. 15:1-13 God's global task will be completed, as He promised in O.T.

Ch. 16:20 Compare to Genesis 3:15.

1 CORINTHIANS

Ch. 1-2 God's unique, saving revelation.

Ch. 3:22-23 All things are yours (in all the earth).

Ch. 4 Trials of Apostles. Remember they are missionaries.

Ch. 5-6 Effect of sexual immorality on witness to world.

Ch. 7 Marriage to unbelievers; celibacy for devotion to the kingdom.

Ch. 8-10 Cultural practices and faithfulness to God.

Ch. 9 Principle of becoming all things to all peoples.

Ch. 12 Unity of Church, despite ethnic and socioeconomic differences.

Ch. 15:30-32, 58 Resurrection justifies all missionary danger and toil.

2 CORINTHIANS

Heartfelt confessions and concerns of Paul the Missionary.

Ch. 1 God comforts those afflicted and persecuted for the Gospel.

Ch. 2:12-5:10 Glory of the New Covenant in weak, human vessels.

Ch. 5:11-6:2 Ambassadors of Christ.
Ch. 6:14-7:1 Separate from the world, in order to be God's people.
Ch. 8-9 Gentile offering for Jerusalem, unity despite ethnic differences.
Ch. 10:3-5 The weapons of our warfare.
Ch. 10:15-16 Local growth, in order to reach "regions beyond".
Ch. 11 Fake apostles; Paul's ministry offered without a price tag.
Ch. 11:22-12:10 Missionary hardships; boasting in weakness.

GALATIANS
Ch. 1 No other Gospel or messenger. Paul called to reach Gentiles.
Ch. 2 Negotiations with other apostles/missionaries.
Ch. 3-4 Gentiles are Abraham's children, not separated by Jewish law.
Ch. 5-6 Freed by Christ to love all people by the Spirit's power.

EPHESIANS
The global nature of the Church. The "mystery of the gospel" is that many peoples are now made into one. Read the letter with this in mind.
Ch. 2 United by Christ despite past divisions and sin; keep the unity.
Ch. 2:1-3,12,19; 4:17-19 The lostness of the Gentiles.
Ch. 1:18 "Power for us who believe..." Power is a key term in Eph.
Ch. 1:14 "For the praise of his glory..." Glory a key term in Gal. also.
Ch. 3:18 The global dimensions of Christ's love.
Ch. 4:11-16 Gifts to help the Church grow in all places and times.
Ch. 6 Spiritual warfare as we invade the Enemy's territory.

PHILIPPIANS
Letter from a missionary to a supportive, mission-minded congregation.
Ch. 1 Preaching of the Gospel during Paul's imprisonment.
Ch. 1:27-2:16 How to testify in Christ-like humility, like stars.
Ch. 2:25-30 Personalized missionary support.
Ch. 3 Pressing on toward the goal.
Ch. 4 Financial support of a missionary.

COLOSSIANS
Ch. 1:6 The Gospel is bearing fruit.
Ch. 1:15ff The Supremacy of Christ.
Ch. 2 God's mystery, Christ in you, overrules all human traditions.
Ch. 4 Prayer, mission, and witness.

> ... at the name of Jesus every knee should bow.
> Phil. 2:10

1 THESSALONIANS
Letter from a missionary to a church he planted. Note the tenderness.
Ch. 1 Thessalonians left idolatry and spread the Gospel in Greece.
Ch. 2-3 Modeling church planting; suffering amid opposition.

2 THESSALONIANS
Ch. 1 Coming judgment for those who do not obey the Gospel.
Ch. 2 The Man of Lawlessness; deception of Satan.
Ch. 3 Pray that the gospel spreads.

1 TIMOTHY

Ch. 1 Paul's conversion: example of God's grace to the worst sinners.
Ch. 2 Prayer urged for all people, whom God wants to be saved.
Ch. 3:16; 4:10 Universal proclamation. Salvation available to all.
Ch. 4 False doctrines and falling away through Satan's influence.
Ch. 6 Riches; applies to cultures swayed by idolatry of materialism.

2 TIMOTHY

Ch. 1 Spirit of power, love and self-discipline to declare grace of God.

Ch. 3-4 End times; evil and false teachers; keep on preaching the truth.

> But God's word is not chained.
> 2 Tim. 2:9

TITUS

Follow-up and discipling. The unorganized church in Crete needed instruction in Christian living as well as warnings against false teachings.
Ch. 2:1-10 The mission is for all generations and classes of believers.
Ch. 2:11ff Salvation offered to all people.
Ch. 3:3-7 Before and after the coming of the gospel.

PHILEMON

Christ changes lives. From jail, Paul begs for amnesty for convert Onesimus. Paul prays Philemon may be active in sharing his faith (v. 6).

HEBREWS

Although there are no direct references to taking the Gospel to others, this book is important for doing mission work, because:
a. The detailed teaching of the Gospel is for all people. The phrase "those who" which occurs often should be understood all-inclusively;
b. The biblical theology of sacrifice is essential for preaching the Gospel to the many people groups which practice sacrifice incorrectly.
c. Hebrews, along with Matthew, is key to Jewish evangelism;
d. The warnings of apostasy and encouragement to endure persecution are needed by all believers in all places who face tribulations.

JAMES

The closing pair of verses (5:19-20) are the only ones which speak specifically of saving sinners. However, James has much advice for those who want outreach efforts to go beyond mere words.
Ch. 1:2ff; 5:10 Trials and suffering.
Ch. 1:11; 5:1ff Warnings to those who trust in riches.
Ch. 2:1ff Warning against favoritism.
Ch. 4:4-6 Friendship with the world.
Ch. 4:7-10 The devil, his tactics, and victory over them.
Ch. 5:1-10 Christ's return and judgment.

1 PETER

Theme: suffering for the sake of Christ.
Ch. 1:1,17; 2:11 Strangers in this world
Ch. 1:18; 2:12, 24; 3:2-7 Living a new, non-pagan lifestyle.
Ch. 2:4-12; 3:1-2, 15-18 Sharing the faith leads to suffering.

2 PETER

Theme: the truth of Peter's Gospel and the danger of false teachers.
Ch. 3 Christ's return; the Lord is patient to call people to repentance.

1 JOHN

In John's spiraling style, several themes appear repeatedly:
a. The truth of God's revelation in Christ and the Apostles' testimony.
b. The whole world as the target of Christ's saving work.
c. The false testimony of antichrists; testing the spirits.
d. Love of the sinful world; overcoming the world.
e. Cosmic victory over the devil.
f. Love for brothers, even not-yet brothers still in need of salvation.

2 JOHN

The devil has sent out false prophets, forces of the antichrist.
Meanwhile, we believers are sent out as forces of the true Christ.

3 JOHN

Our attitude toward supporting messengers and missionaries of the truth.

JUDE

False teachers promote all kinds of lies. The truth is that the Lord will come to judge everyone. So snatch people from the fire while there is time.

REVELATION

Portrays the global war between the hordes of Satan and the forces of God. The theme is: God wins! In Revelation's spiraling style, words like testimony, witness, overcome, world, kings, tribe, tongue, people, and nation repeat often.
Ch. 1; 5; 11:15; 17:14; 19 Divine identity and global authority of Christ.
Ch. 2-3; 6:9-10; 12:10-11; 14:13 Suffering, persecution, overcoming.
Ch. 7:9; 11:9; 13:7; 14:6; 15:4; 20:3 God and Satan compete for control over every tribe, tongue, people, and nation.
Ch. 2-3; 9:20-21; 12-13; 16:14-21:8; 22:15 Satanic deception, idols, magic, false teachers.
Ch. 17-18 Plagues, judgment; Fall of Babylon.
Ch. 19-22 Victory!
Ch. 21:24-26 Final victorious reference to nations and kings.
Ch. 22:17 Final invitation to the world: "The Spirit and the bride say, 'Come!' And let him who hears say, 'Come!' Whoever is thirsty, let him come; and whoever wishes, let him take the free gift of the water of life."

SCRIPTURE INDEX

About the Author

During over 20 years of ministry, Dr. Phil Bickel has worked as a:
- church planter and parish pastor
- missionary and media writer/producer in Venezuela
- professor of evangelism and missions
- pastor of evangelism and missions

Finally, Phil discovered what he wanted to be when he grew up: an Outreach Encourager. What's that? Someone who helps Christians overcome fears, doubts, and inertia, so they joyfully share their faith. Phil can serve you as a writer, speaker, or consultant. He will:
- communicate profound biblical truths in everyday terms
- teach your audience to share Christ in sensitive, relevant ways
- motivate your audience with God's promises
- provide practical advice that really works

His favorite speaking and writing topics include:
- Outreach Promises: God's encouragement for sharing your faith
- The Power of Y'All: the joys of Christian teamwork
- New Creeds for Today's Needs: making your witness relevant
- Creating Outreach Strategies: leave old ruts, build new bridges
- Considering a Church Career?: answers to your questions
- All the World Is in All the Word: outreach themes in the Bible
- Witnessing Can Be Fun: the joys of friendship evangelism
- Rock Foundations: rock music history from a Christian viewpoint

His credentials include:
- Ordained pastor of the Lutheran Church-Missouri Synod
- D. of Missiology degree, Trinity Ev. Divinity School, Deerfield, IL
- Author of over twenty titles about evangelism and missions
- Member of the Evangelical Missiological Society
- Member of the Lutheran Society for Missiology

You can contact Phil Bickel by:
- Mail: 1167 Ryan Avenue W., Roseville, MN 55113-5929
- Telephone: 651-487-1260
- E-mail: pmbickel@aol.com

ORDER FORM

You may return undamaged items for a refund, within 1 year.
All prices are postage paid. All shipments must be prepaid.
Prices are in U.S. dollars and must be paid in U.S. dollars.

Name: _____

Address: _____

City: _____

State/Province: _____ Postal Code: _____ Country: _____

Tel.: _____ Fax: _____ E-mail: _____

Ship to (if different than above):

Name: _____

Address: _____

City: _____

State/Province: _____ Postal Code: _____ Country: _____

Tel.: _____ Fax: _____ E-mail: _____

Price Schedule

Quantity of Order:	Discount:	Item Price
1-2 books	0% off	$8.95 (Insert in "Price" blank below)
3-199	40% off	$5.37 (Insert in "Price" blank below)
200 & up	50% off	$4.48 (Insert in "Price" blank below)

Please send the following:

TITLE	QUANTITY	x	PRICE	=	AMOUNT
Outreach Promises	_____	x	_____	=	$_____

Add 6.5% sales tax for shipments to Minnesota: $_____

Add Handling: $___3.50

TOTAL: $_____

Make check or money order payable to: Roller Coaster Press.

____ Check enclosed   ____ Money order enclosed

Credit card: ____ Visa ____ Mastercard

Card number: _____ Exp. date: _____

On-line orders: ppco@cpuinc.net
Telephone orders: 888-222-0161
Fax orders: 616-925-6057
Mail orders: Attn.: Therese Ferrell, Patterson Printing,
1550 Territorial Rd., Benton Harbor, MI 49022

TITLES BY THE AUTHOR

Outreach Promises:
God's Encouragement for Sharing Your Faith

The Lord never intended to burden you with witnessing guilt and fears. Instead, He peppered the Bible with outreach promises to lift your sights and renew your vision for the lost. Find out how to identify and apply these promises to your life. Group Discussion Guide included.

Order from your local bookstore or Roller Coaster Press. See Order Form on next page.   ISBN 0-9663765-0-1   112 pp. $8.95 ppd.

The Goal of the Gospel:
God's Purpose in Saving You

God saved and equipped you for a purpose. Have you discovered it? An eye-opening view of Romans as Paul the Missionary intended it to be understood. Ideal for lay Bible studies. Co-author: Robert L. Nordlie.

Order from your local book store or Concordia Publishing House (1-800-325-3040).   ISBN 0-570-04569-X   272 pp. $14.95

Considering a Church Career?:
Determining God's Plan for Your Life

Looking for career counseling regarding church work? Here it is. Answers questions commonly asked by youth and by adults seeking a new career. Directs you from the "just toying" stage to concrete actions. Co-author: Curtis Deterding.

Order from your local book store or Concordia Publishing House (1-800-325-3040).   ISBN 0-570-04850-8   64 pp. $3.50

Outreach Encourager Web Site

Visit Phil Bickel's web site where you will find:
- More details about the above titles
- Information about his favorite speaking topics
- Excerpts, articles, and dramas on outreach subjects
- Lots of free, down-loadable stuff

URL: http://www.christianlink.com/evangelism/encourager.

ORDER FORM

**You may return undamaged items for a refund, within 1 year.
All prices are postage paid. All shipments must be prepaid.
Prices are in U.S. dollars and must be paid in U.S. dollars.**

Name: _____

Address: _____

City: _____

State/Province: _____ Postal Code: _____ Country: _____

Tel.: _____ Fax: _____ E-mail: _____

Ship to (if different than above):

Name: _____

Address: _____

City: _____

State/Province: _____ Postal Code: _____ Country: _____

Tel.: _____ Fax: _____ E-mail: _____

TITLES	RETAIL(1-2)	DISCOUNT(3+)	QTY.	AMOUNT	
Outreach Promises	$ 9.99	$ 5.99	x ____	= $_____	
Fishing for Souls	$11.99	$ 9.59	x ____	= $_____	ielow)
New Creeds for Today's Needs	$ 2.95	$ 2.35	x ____	= $_____	ielow) ielow)
Joy to the World	$12.99	$10.39	x ____	= $_____	
Considering a Church Career?	$ 5.99	$ 4.79	x ____	= $_____	

                                    Sub-total: $_____

Add 6.5% sales tax for shipments to Minnesota: $_____   —

                        Add handling: $__3.50   —

Discount prices apply to any   **TOTAL:** $_____   0
combination of 3 or more books.   —

Make check or money order payable to: Roller Coaster Press.

Telephone orders: 1-888-894-1594

E-mail orders: order@rollercoasterpress.com

Mail orders: Roller Coaster Press,
9513 Stanley Avenue S., Bloomington, MN 55437-2048   _____

Read *God's Mission Promises*, a free weekly e-column available at www.lcmsworldmission.org/mp. To subscribe send a blank e-mail to mission.promises-subscribe@listbot.com.

ing,
49022

Visit www.rollercoasterpress.com for more evangelism and mission resources by Philip Bickel.